Publisher Michael Summers
Editor Arnold Sherman
Designer David Eyres

Tel Aviv-Jaffa

Published by Sterling Publications Limited, on the occasion of the 40th anniversary of the establishment of the State of Israel, under the auspices of The Municipality of Tel Aviv-Jaffa, The Chamber of Commerce of Tel Aviv-Jaffa, and The Tel Aviv-Jaffa Hotels and Tourism Association.

Sterling Publications Limited is a subsidiary of The Sterling Publishing Group PLC, Garfield House, 86–88 Edgware Road, London W2 2YW

Issued free of charge to members of the Chamber of Commerce of Tel Aviv-Jaffa, Heads of Governments and senior government ministers and Presidents and Chief Executives of leading American and European companies who have trade and commercial links with Tel Aviv and Israel as a whole.

ISBN 0–902570–32–3

Printed in England by Drogher Press, Christchurch, Dorset

Contents

Old Jaffa seen from Tel Aviv.

Foreword

I had just returned from a visit to a Greek island off the coast of Turkey when my eldest daughter phoned, informing me that a London publisher had been seeking me. Before long, and thanks to satellite-assisted telephone communications, I found out about Sterling Publications Limited, and its intention to publish a book about Tel Aviv during Israel's 40th anniversary celebrations in 1988. The news certainly interested me and I was more than happy to vault to London two days later for "some preliminary talks".

But it wasn't really "the talks" which excited me. Although involved in journalism and printing for the past 35 years, I had rarely been exposed to the type of editorial and production quality that is intrinsic to all the works produced by Sterling. There was no tendency to skimp or compromise. All the editions were characterized by full color, the best chrome paper, and exacting editing. I was delighted that Sterling had decided to bring out its first book about Israel, recalling the ancient Hebrew adage: "Let foreigners, and not yourself, praise you" — and that I was being offered the position of editor.

Having written so many books and articles about Israel, it occurred to me that it would have been a good deal easier to produce the volume myself and not resort to commissioning writers. On the other hand, I realized that here was an opportunity to mobilize the finest specialists in the country to write about the topics that interested them, and their future readers, the most. After agreeing on the basic parameters and deadlines of the project, Sterling's managing director, Michael Summers — whose brainchild the project was from inception — gave me a totally free hand to assemble the best coterie of writers available, and to gather the necessary artwork which would be essential for the book to achieve the quality level demanded by Sterling.

I have worked with many photographers during my numerous years in journalism and literature, and I knew that the success of the project was dependent on finding the right man for the exacting chore of adequately and sensitively covering the multifaceted aspects of Tel Aviv. The man I chose, Yigal Zaken, a young Jerusalemite whose work had been appearing regularly in top quality Israeli and European journals, more than met my expectations. He worked tirelessly, week after week, to assemble the necessary slides and photos, often toiling around the clock so that he could "capture the right light".

All the writers who were subsequently assigned to

cover stories were top professionals, many of whom I had known and worked closely with for years. Michal Yudelman and Helen Kaye of the *Jerusalem Post* had been successfully covering the Tel Aviv scene for years. Joe Morgenstern was certainly one of the ranking economic writers in the country and Suzy David had authored a couple of the most successful recipe books ever produced in Israel. As is often the case, one writer led to another. Paul Hirschhorn and I had been working together for years on high technology subjects. Having covered the diamond industry extensively in the past, it was obvious that he was the right man to write about that topic in our book. But Paul not only made the expected contribution, he also led us to Gordon Shifman, who wrote a superlative piece on Tel Aviv University and Bar Ilan.

In scouring for material, we also had a little luck. Ruth Bondy's piece on Dizengoff and Shlomo Shva's excellent reportage on Jaffa were reprints from El Al's inflight magazine and were superbly geared to our needs. Ruth, whom I have known and appreciated for almost a quarter of a century, is undisputably one of the top Hebrew writers in the country. The two freelance journalists, Jordan Roberts and Jeremy Kitling, who covered the vital subjects of tourism and culture, have appeared in some of the most prestigious travel magazines in the United States. It was a pleasure to add them to our own roster.

While there was never any dispute about the future quality of the book or the themes of the tome, one piquant difference of opinion was spelling. Is it "centre" or "center", and what about "colour" or "color"? Happily, not only did our British publishers not pull rank, but they were easily amenable to American spelling, as indeed a high proportion of readers would undoubtedly originate from the far side of the Atlantic.

A complicated, new project like a high quality book needs more than sympathy and enthusiasm. It requires a lot of legwork and support. Ami Federman, whose family pioneered the largest and most important hotel complex in the country — the Dan chain — was not only an early advocate, but, as head of the Tel Aviv Hotel Association, provided yeoman service for this project. We were also most fortunate that the Tel Aviv Chamber of Commerce, an organization which has done so much to promote the city, was enthusiastically there when we needed it.

My penultimate note is that there is a certain amount of leadtime between the compilation and writing of an article and the publication of a book. So there is always the chance that museum hours will vary, prices will change a bit and a zany café which just opened has since closed. The micro may vary a bit, but not the macro — which is just another way of saying: Dream City, Israel.

With all this in mind, there is very little left to say except "welcome to Tel Aviv."

Arnold Sherman
Editor

About the Editor

Arnold Sherman arrived in Israel exactly 25 years ago after having served as news editor of the prestigious American magazine, Aviation Week and Space Technology, for six years. His first position in Israel was public relations head of Israel Aircraft Industries which subsequently became the largest industrial complex in the country. He moved to El Al in 1965 where he remained until the end of 1982, starting as company spokesman and ending his career there as Vice President. Sherman then moved to Haifa where he was Executive Vice Chairman of Technion University until the tail end of 1986.

In addition to authoring hundreds of articles and acting as correspondent for major newspapers in the United States, Europe and Israel, Sherman has published 24 books which run the spectrum from poetry to high technology. He penned five travel books in which he wrote extensively, naturally, about Tel Aviv.

Now working on a new writing project, Sherman shares his time between Israel and Greece.

About the Photography Editor

Yigal Zaken is a young Israeli photographer whose works have consistently appeared in major publications both in Israel and abroad. Nearly all the color photos appearing in this book were taken by him personally.

A city in his own image

EVERY Friday night, thousands of Jerusalem residents hop into their cars and clog the westbound highway heading for Tel Aviv. They all want a taste of the shining lights and hectic nightlife that only this city can offer. On the outskirts of the city they are joined by tens of thousands from the suburbs, intent on the same objective. Tel Avivians are wont to say — and they believe it, too — that the best thing about Jerusalem is the fast road to Tel Aviv!

Tel Aviv is Israel's center of culture, business, entertainment and nightlife. Although its population numbers less than 350 000, it caters to more than a million commuters a day, who come to work, do business, shop, dine and have a good time in the city. A bustling, vibrant city that lives in the fast lane and never shuts down, with an intense, lively entertainment and cultural scene, Tel Aviv may be said to reflect the image of its mayor for the past 15 years — Shlomo Lahat.

"When I started raising funds abroad for Tel Aviv years ago, people would say: 'Tel Aviv? Isn't that the place near the airport? But it's disgusting, ugly, dirty'," Lahat recalls.

"Today, it's a city with culture, entertainment, business and beauty. It's a popular place to live and the shortage of housing here proves it. Everyone — young and old — wants to live in Tel Aviv. The city has much

Tel Aviv author *Michal Yudelman* **talks to the city's charismatic, controversial and candid mayor, Shlomo Lahat.**

Right: Kikar Malhei Israel is the city's town hall center.
Far right top: the view from City Hall.
Far right bottom: Tel Aviv's charismatic mayor, Shlomo Lahat.

to offer and the general standard of living here is high. Also, it's becoming more convenient to live right in the city rather than commute, because of the heavy traffic coming in and out all day long."

Describing the difference between the effervescent Tel Aviv social scene and that of Jerusalem, Lahat cannot resist telling one of his favorite jokes: What do Jerusalemites do for a hot night on the town? They go out and have a nice dinner, go dancing, meet friends for beer, perhaps see a show — then rush home in time to see Erev Hadash (a television program put out at 5pm) — and toddle off to bed. It was Lahat who insisted, resisting heavy pressure from religious groups and political factions, that cinemas, nightclubs and restaurants remain open on Friday nights. So while other cities rolled up their sidewalks every Friday afternoon with the approach of the Sabbath, Tel Aviv throbbed and sparkled and danced all night.

Lahat encouraged the building of shopping malls and highrises and completed the seaside promenade, which brought life to the decrepit southern part of town. Now a renovated, variegated line of restaurants and cafés, the road along the promenade is open and full of patrons until the small hours of the night. In a word, Lahat dragged Tel Aviv, kicking and screaming, from provincialism into the vulgar glitter and sophistication of an ultra modern, twentieth century city.

While the mayor has many admirers and supporters, he certainly does not lack critics. He is held responsible for neglecting the city's slum quarters in favor of exhibitionist projects; for allowing the gracious old quarters of the city's founders to crumble and collapse in disrepair; for truncating meals-on-wheels programs for old people and dental services for needy children — while never sparing expenses for vast outdoor concerts given by the Israel Philharmonic Orchestra or for fireworks on Independence Day.

Criticism notwithstanding, Lahat has that quality which puts him way ahead in the race for mayor — charisma. For no matter how arrogant or errant he might be, no political party has anyone who can compete with him in the municipal arena. A decade and a half as mayor of Israel's most cosmopolitan city has left Lahat with few political illusions (he failed in one attempt to reach the Knesset, and again, where he tried to set up a new Liberal Center party), but with a stronger sense of his public image. Sometimes described as being his own best public relations man, he enjoys publicity and is not beyond manufacturing a scandal to attract attention. In fact, he once admitted in a newspaper interview that this was the only way to get things done in Israel — that is, to pressure the government into allocating more money for the city.

He shares the mercurialism of New York Mayor Ed

Rooftop view from the historic Neve Zedek neighborhood which is being tastefully restored.

The measure of any metropolis is how it attends to the old. These are the other faces of a city which will soon celebrate its eightieth birthday.

Koch and appears to emulate Jerusalem Mayor Teddy Kollek, by personally venturing overseas to raise funds for Tel Aviv and by hosting public events. Despite Tel Aviv's undeniable problems, like having too many cars and inadequate public sanitation, Lahat generally likes what he sees. Envisioning the city's future from his twelfth-storey office at City Hall, he says: "I don't want to change Tel Aviv's vitality, liveliness, or aggressiveness. I don't want it to lose its centrality. I'd hate Tel Aviv to turn into some nice, quiet, green, Washington-like town.

"Let Tel Aviv retain the place it holds in Israel today. Let Jaffa become one continuity with the city and let many more people come to live in Tel Aviv. A city needs residents to keep it vital and alive. I would like Tel Aviv to have about 500 000 inhabitants. Otherwise it will turn into an industrial and business center that dies when people go home in the afternoon. I want people to live here and enjoy it."

The slum quarters, in Lahat's Tel Aviv of the future, will disappear. Jaffa's flea market, Jerusalem Boulevard, the older Manshia, Florentin and Shapira quarters will all be renovated and rehabilitated and will attract tourists. The most successful example of this, Lahat notes, is the Heart of Tel Aviv project, which aims to renovate the city's old central area. He intends to do the same for other areas, transforming slum quarters into attractive residential areas.

14

Life in the city (from top to bottom): some soldiers relax in the shade; a Jaffa flea market stallholder takes a break from hawking his wares; and shoppers hustle and bustle in the Carmel Food Market.

At the same time, Lahat is encouraging luxury areas replete with skyscrapers: "I mean Tel Avivian skyscrapers, with, say, 20 floors, not 100. In a city where land is so valuable there is no alternative to living high up."

Tomorrow's Tel Aviv must have a commuter train and an efficient transport system — either an underground subway, or a monorail, or electric trams. "It must happen in the next 25 to 50 years. The Dan Bus Cooperative which services Tel Aviv simply cannot provide efficient public transport." And the beachfront, Lahat says, must remain low-built and accessible to retain the city's Mediterranean character. He envisages the city forging ahead in even a bigger way as Israel's business, culture, financial and political center — to become the "Manhattan of the Middle East".

Lahat wants history to remember him for three main achievements: rehabilitation of the needy quarters, developing the beachfront and the life it brought to the entire southern part of town, and the Golda Arts Center — which, when completed, will be the city's opera, theater, concert and ballet nexus — a sort of Israeli Lincoln Center. "And greenery. I want the city to turn green. If it were up to me, I'd tear half the buildings down and build parks instead. I'm going to demolish Magen David Adom House on Maze Street, the Teachers Union Building on Dizengoff and the defunct A D Gordon School structure on Bernstein Street and build parks there."

Tel Aviv's most aggravating problems, as Lahat sees them, are the inability of young couples to afford living in the city, the plight of Arab and Jewish residents in Jaffa, the lack of old age homes, street litter and traffic congestion.

"I feel I must find a solution for the young people and families draining out of Tel Aviv. I can't offer gifts, but I want to provide young couples with subsidized loans so they can buy apartments in town. I want to increase the building percentage in neighborhoods north of the Yarkon River."

Lahat continues: "Another thing I must do is to rehabilitate Jaffa for both Jews and Arabs. They're equally citizens of Israel. As for the elderly, I'm contemplating a package deal in which old folks who need supervision will sell their apartments to young couples and ensure their future in high-class old folks homes. Cleanliness is a well-known, acute problem. But I have plans which will bring about a major change in the city's cleanliness situation within a year."

Asked about his future as mayor, Lahat is confident of his ability to remain in that position for the time being. "I want to serve this city as long as I am strong and able. As soon as I feel that I'm languishing on my past successes, I'll stand down. I want to make one thing clear: I have no intention of growing old in the mayor's seat." □

Michal Yudelman is a feature writer for the Jerusalem Post and also works as an editor for Metro, a regional paper specializing in Tel Aviv.

Hill of Spring

THE most extraordinary feature of Tel Aviv is that it exists at all! The first Jewish metropolis to be built in 2000 years does not have the historical and religious legacies of Jerusalem, the nation's capital. It doesn't boast the natural advantages of Haifa with its deep water harbor and verdant scenery. Tel Aviv is not poised on an ancient crossroad like Beersheva — nor is it a geopolitical asset like Eilat. More a story of people than artifacts, Israel's commercial and banking center is really a uniquely Jewish paradox which absolutely refuses to be defined, categorized or inhibited.

It is brash, tempestuous and even anarchic. Yet this city is certainly also gentle and hospitable. Ask a Tel Avivian for directions on a Friday afternoon and, more often than not, you will be invited home for *kreplach* and chicken that very evening. Inform a taxi driver that you come from London or New York and not only will your genealogy be traced, but a kindred relationship might even be uncovered. Mention politics to a casual acquaintance, and you can expect a two-hour dissertation on Hebrew Machiavellism capped with coffee and *strudel* in one of those indigenous cafés which simply refuses to sleep.

The city comprising both Tel Aviv and Jaffa is outrageously and unashamedly different. There is no single, ecological pattern present, but rather a confluence — a melding of cultures, enterprises and demography.

More than anything else, Tel Aviv-Jaffa is a strip of Mediterranean coastline whose population of 327 000 reaches to over one and a half million, which includes the satellite suburbs of Ramat Aviv, Ramat Gan, Givatayim, Holon and Bat Yam feeding on the commerce, culture and cacophony of the nation's second largest concentration of frenetic Israelis.

If the magnificent, sandy beaches tend to be overcrowded during summer weekends, they are also protected by well-engineered breakwaters that drastically reduce the possibilities of intrepid swimmers being sucked out to Piraeus or swept down to Alexandria. There is a fine marina smack in the middle of the Tel Aviv-Jaffa tourist center which is worth more than a precursory examination if, for no other reason, than to observe the number of characters who gravitate toward the sea.

The hotel strip, along Hayarkon Street, is probably one of the country's most familiar tourist sites. Grand five-star hotels stretch for a mile along the land adjacent to the sea. The scene is noisy and competitive, with the Hilton dominating the landscape from a bluff headland to the north to the more venerable Dan Hotel providing flank to the south. As for what lies in between, you name it and it's there — the Sheraton, Ramada, Plaza, *et al.*

However, the real attraction of the coastal strip is much more than sand and concrete. The atmosphere, highlighted by some of the best restaurants in the country and by dozens of boutiques and art galleries, is international, exciting and vibrant. The linguistic ambience is pure polyglot; Hebrew and English dominates, but there's enough Yiddish, German,

The story of Tel Aviv-Jaffa is much more than the chronicle of a city, according to this book's editor and long-term Israeli resident and writer, *Arnold Sherman*. **It is a uniquely Jewish paradox which absolutely refuses to be defined.**

Tel Aviv-Jaffa seen from the Shalom Tower, the country's tallest building.

17

French and Japanese to rival the ancient city of Babel. The tasteful esplanade running all the way down to the fringes of Jaffa and the huge Dan Panorama Hotel equally attracts sightseers and citizens. There are young soldiers and older gigolos. There are visiting archeologists and local bankers. There are politicians preparing the ploys of tomorrow mixing with Scandinavian sunbathers blissfully incinerating the outer layers of their Nordic skin.

There is a great deal more to Tel Aviv-Jaffa, however, than tourism and beaches. Culture is a very serious business indeed. Almost within touching distance of each other, for example, just off Ibn Gvirol Avenue, are three of the country's most exciting cultural centers. The Mann Auditorium was founded in 1936 to attract and employ the hundreds of excellent musicians and performers who came as refugees from Europe. Home base for the Israel Philharmonic, it has hosted such celebrities as Toscanini, Bernstein, Haifetz and Menuhin and has been under the musical directorship of Zubin Mehta since 1969.

Next door to the Mann Auditorium is the Habima National Theater, which was originally founded in Moscow in 1918 and moved to Palestine a decade later to play a key role in the renaissance of Hebrew drama. And the Helen Rubenstein Art Pavilion features Israeli and international artistic renditions and is part of the Tel Aviv Museum complex.

Jaffa's refurbished artists' quarter overlooking both the sea and Tel Aviv is another of the country's most distinctive attractions. The streets are narrow and cobblestoned. There is an ancient archeological excavation located in the middle of the complex which abounds with boutiques, galleries and fine restaurants. The atmosphere is arty and romantic — one more indication of what the city is all about.

The area has two notable seats of learning: Tel Aviv University in Ramat Aviv, and Bar Ilan University, which is actually in Ramat Gan. These superb institutions service the needs of the Israeli megapolis and its environs, ministering to tens of thousands of graduates and undergraduates each year — as well as to

visiting students from all over the world.

The recurring message of the city is people. Near the colorful Carmel fruit and vegetable market close to the old boundaries between Tel Aviv and Jaffa is the Yemenite Quarter, inhabited by an older generation of people who thought they were being brought to the Promised Land "on the wings of eagles" — and younger citizens, who are the land's computer specialists, chemists, and political leaders.

Only an invisible hairline from Tel Aviv proper is Bnai Braq. This is an ultra-orthodox district, with some of the most serious *yeshivas* in the country. The citizens are sober, sedate and serious. Yet girls can be seen wearing short shorts and very negligible blouses only a couple of streets away in a less traditional neighborhood.

There is an enclave of former South Africans in Tel Aviv where, even after 40 years, the oldtimers prefer to express themselves in Johannesburg English rather than Ben-Yehudian Hebrew. There is a building complex once erected exclusively for pilots and now pretty

Two years after the decision to establish Tel Aviv and one year before the formal move into the sandy wasteland adjacent to Jaffa, the city's founders meet officially for the first time at the site in 1908 (top right).
They were an extraordinary collection of men and women who were fervently committed to the proposition that not only would a Jewish city emerge from the site, but that a homeland would one day be established. A year after the enclave was formally established, Jewish pioneers (above left) can be seen carting soil over the sands in 1910. The western part of Rothschild Boulevard already begins to emerge in 1911 (centre). Huts anchored in sand in 1934 was the beginning of Tel Aviv's most famous thoroughfare, Dizengoff Street (bottom).

much inhabited by more terrestrial creatures. There are places in Tel Aviv, just off Dizengoff Square, where the *lingua franca* is Yiddish, not Hebrew — and where *farfel* is still preferred to *falafel*. There are streets in the Hatikva Section where everyone's father was a Moroccan and places still so Rumanian that only the gypsy violinists are missing.

Whatever Tel Aviv-Jaffa may or may not be, one cannot deny its extraordinarily implicit role in the establishment of modern Israel. While the country proudly celebrates its 40th anniversary this year, the first Jewish city in modern times retains a history almost twice that long. Certainly it is no exaggeration to maintain that, without Tel Aviv or its equivalent, there would have been no Jewish state.

Jews were already living in the port city of Jaffa in the late nineteenth century, although the slumbering town with its makeshift, shallow harbor, was predominantly Arab in population and flavor throughout the Turkish Ottoman occupation. As a tiny minority, the Jews were susceptible to the moods and mercurial reactions of their neighbors which frequently fluctuated from indifference to downright hostility. There were some bitter pogroms and an air of uncertainty which demonstrated just how vulnerable the Jews were.

The Jews also acknowledged that Jaffa was not ideal for their families. The streets were crowded and dirty. Houses were at a premium. The air was fetid and parents worried about the health of their children.

With a boost from the Jewish National Fund, which was charged with the task of acquiring land in the country for future settlement, a nucleus of Jaffa families began examining the possibilities of a Jewish suburb on the northern outskirts of the city in 1906. The land was pure sand, but the idea of a strictly Jewish, yet airier and more defensible, enclave that would be near enough to Jaffa for work, shopping and urban accoutrements was an appealing alternative. Three years later, 32 acres of bleached sand dunes were acquired — and 60 families, numbering 250 people, prepared for the short trek north under the leadership of Meir Dizengoff.

A fine photograph of the city's pioneers exists. It shows determined, steadfast faces and a great deal of Victorian clothing which must have been unbearable to wear in the sultry heat of the treeless beachfront property. In his invocation address Dizengoff caused a considerable amount of amusement when he prophesised that the settlement, which was named Tel Aviv — the "Hill of Spring" — would one day reach a population of 25 000. This seemed unthinkable at the time; water was at a premium, roads did not exist and the land was deemed hopeless for growing anything.

Despite all their problems, the main civic goal of the pioneering families was to set up a high school, the first ever to emerge in Palestine. Whatever else might happen, the children would be assured a top-level education; the Herzlia Gymnasium — originally planned to resemble Solomon's Temple but actually emerging more like an Ottoman fortress — was designed and built while most families were still living in tents and shacks.

If the first public building was named Herzlia, it followed naturally that the initial thoroughfare would be called Rechov Herzl, each place named for Theodor Herzl, the founder of political Zionism. As home began to emerge from the sand and a semblance of order arose out of chaos, relations with the Jaffa Arabs worsened. Land was a constant source of dispute. On the one hand, the previous landowners enjoyed the cash received for the purchase of what was then deemed useless property; on the other, they resented the flourishing offspring mushrooming out of the northern edges of town. By the time World War I broke out five years later, there were already 3000 Jews living in Tel Aviv and demand for land far exceeded supply. The reason for this was obvious: with the exception of a few lonely settlements in the north, which were precariously trying to survive, the only independent Jewish enclave in the country was Tel Aviv.

The ruling Turks never readily understood Jewish aspirations; they were not oppressors, but were certainly not sympathizers. When World War I erupted, one of the first official Ottoman acts was to dispossess the Jews of Tel Aviv, as they regarded the coastline as a strategic zone. The war ended and the Jews returned;

Above: Lord Balfour (center, foreground) visits the city in 1925.
Below: Tel Aviv's first mayor, Meir Dizengoff (center, foreground), chats with Swedish Crown Prince Gustav Adolph in December 1934.

CHANGING FACES OF TEL AVIV-JAFFA

Considering its relative youth, Tel Aviv-Jaffa has an astonishing number of architectural facades to beguile, bedevil and bemuse. In an attempt to preserve some of the older architecture of the city, major efforts were made in the older Neve Zedek neighborhood to retain the stately beauty that once characterized the city. The Jaffa artists' quarter (bottom right) famous for its paintings, boutiques and nightlife, has been tastefully reconstructed.

Great Britain replaced Turkey as the occupational power in Palestine, and the Balfour Declaration gave credence and hope to all Jews aspiring to a Jewish homeland.

By 1921, Tel Aviv boasted 15 000 residents and was officially recognized as a city independent from Jaffa. The first mayor to be elected was the same Meir Dizengoff who had presided over the settlement from the beginning, and the Biblical motto adopted for the lively community was "I shall build thee and thou shalt be built". It was appropriate; more and more Jews were flocking to their ancestral homeland despite severe immigration restrictions, difficult economic problems, and worsening relations with the Arabs — which often resulted in ugly bloodbaths.

By 1925 Tel Aviv had reached a population of 34 000,

was engaged in massive construction and was creating the nucleus for a revived Hebrew culture. Shops and small industries were emerging all the time. The indigenous Zionist movement was quartered in the burgeoning city with David Ben-Gurion assiduously preparing the way for an eventual Jewish homeland. While reclamation of the land was still a national priority, many of the new immigrants were not suited for agrarian life. At a time when Jerusalem was still a sleepy, religious settlement in the Judean Mountains, Haifa was mostly Arab and the Negev was almost utterly inaccessible.

As Tel Aviv grew, relations with neighboring Jaffa worsened. No Jew could feel comfortable or safe in the ancient port city which teemed with Arab nationalists who, by the 1930s, were being fuelled and encouraged

The city flourished and grew beyond all expectations with refugees and Zionists arriving throughout the twenties and thirties. A typical face of young Tel Aviv was the newspaper vendor selling foreign and local papers in 1934 (left). Another aspect of Tel Aviv was the "beadle" announcing the arrival of the Sabbath in 1935 (centre). Hatware borrowed from the previous Ottoman rulers of the country, short trousers adopted from the British, a Jewish auxiliary policeman directs traffic in 1936 (right).

by Nazi agents interested equally in undermining the English and exterminating the Jews. But there were Jewish nationalists as well. Tel Aviv became the clandestine center for activities aimed at the eventual expulsion of the British and the creation of a Jewish homeland. The Haganah was engaged in training and arms procurement as a prelude to what was already regarded as an inevitable struggle, while activities of the Palmach, the strike force of the *kibbutzim*, were coordinated in the city. Under the impatient orchestration of Menahem Begin, Etzel established cells underground in Tel Aviv that ruthlessly attacked British military installations and repaid Arab terror with terror. And the Tel Aviv-based Lehi was active as well, striking fiercely against the increasingly adamant occupiers.

"It was a very difficult period," recalled veteran Tel Avivian, Haim Cohen, caught in the national anguish. "The rise of Nazism gave new urgency to the requirement for unrestricted immigration into the country. No one could foresee how terrible the plight of Europe's Jews would eventually become, but it was already apparent, just before World War II, that the Jews would be the main sufferers. All of us had relations and families in Europe and all of us were terrified.

"In retrospect, I can understand that the British had their own set of problems and priorities. Certainly, they didn't want to alienate the Arabs, but they miscalculated badly. Jews flocked to their banners. The Arabs were either neutral or pro-German.

"And then there was so much divisiveness among the Jews themselves. Brothers ceased to speak to each other. Friends fought one against the other. Whole families were torn by irreconcilable political philosophies. It was a most terrible period — for the world, for the Jews of Palestine, for Tel Aviv."

Hava Mendelson was 16 years old in 1947 when the United Nations called for the partition of Palestine and the creation of an independent Jewish homeland. "I cannot possible describe the emotions we experienced. Our small apartment off Rechov Allenby was overflowing with friends and relations who were listening to the radio with us. Outside, I could see British patrols and armored personnel carriers moving up and down the street since they expected trouble no matter what happened, although they were fairly certain that the Mandate would be authorized to continue. When the vote began, I felt that my chest would explode with excitement. I was cradling my baby sister and involuntarily squeezed her so hard that she cried. My father, never a very emotional person, was sipping tea quietly in the corner of the living room when suddenly he began to cry. 'Don't cry, papa', I hugged him, 'we are going to win'. 'I know,' he said, 'that's why I'm crying. It is from happiness'.

"Soon we were all crying and hugging each other. Papa, who had never drunk anything stronger than sabbath wine in his life, brought out a bottle of cognac and everybody was toasting l'chaim to each other while we laughed and cried and kissed.

"We younger people were so exuberant we couldn't stand the physical restraints of the apartment so we spilled out into the street, where it seemed that tens of thousands of other youngsters had the same idea. Before long there was accordion music and *horas* being danced. Motor traffic had ceased. Nobody could get

HALLELUIAH EL AL!

Halleluiah! An international word, so often heard by El Al's crew at the end of a flight — an exclamation made by passengers who are not necessarily Israeli, or Jewish.
As a matter of fact, 63% of all El Al passengers are not Israelis. They select El Al because of service and performance, and confirm their satisfaction not just verbally, but also in

numerous letters. That's why it came as no surprise that when the English periodical WHICH conducted an extensive survey among 15,000 travelers, asking them which airline they prefer, El Al was selected as one of the top 5 international airline carriers out of a list of 40. Halleluiah El Al!

EL AL אל על

CHANGING FACES OF TEL AVIV-JAFFA
Many beautiful buildings have been preserved. One of Tel Aviv's most unforgettable sights is this cheesecake concoction in the center of the Hayarkon Street tourist center (top left).

through. I had never seen Tel Aviv so joyous before. I had never seen the people so hopeful, so grateful, so determined.

"I noticed that a British corporal was watching us. He had a nice face and seemed very much alone and on that day I loved all of humanity. 'Come dance with us,' I suggested. 'I don't understand the Jews,' he said. 'By next year you will all be dead.'"

When Israel's War of Independence erupted a year later, there were 210 000 citizens in the coastal city. Fierce fighting broke out between Arab Jaffa and Jewish Tel Aviv even before the Jewish state was formally proclaimed in Tel Aviv on May 14. The area adjacent to the two cities was pulverized by mortar and light arms fire while Jaffa's civilian population was systematically replaced by Arab irregulars. Of the 100 000 residents of the Arab city, only 4000 remained during the warring summer of 1948. The rest fled under promises from their own religious and political leadership that they would be returning shortly not only to their former tenements in Jaffa, but to the new villas abounding in Tel Aviv. It didn't quite work out that way.

The war ended victoriously for Israel and the sluice gates of immigration were immediately opened. First, there were the concentration camp survivors who had to be rescued and provided with homes, jobs and medical treatment. Then there were Jews in the Arab countries who were under threat of annihilation if they weren't moved out quickly. Tel Aviv opened its gates, its heart and its pocket book, swelling its population while successive waves of new immigrants slowly began resettling mostly deserted Jaffa. By the 1950s, there were already over 65 000 Jews living in the old port city. After a while, the borders were too artificial to exist and a merger of the cities was as inevitable as once had been their separation.

Although the capital of the country was Jerusalem,

Horse-drawn carriages on the sprawling seafront in 1935.

An early photo of the Allenby-Shenkin and King George crossroads.

almost all the important government offices were in Tel Aviv throughout the early statehood days in the 1950s and the early 1960s. Tel Aviv was the undisputed business center of the country. It was head office for all the major banks; the hub of export activities; a center for art, drama and publishing. Every major Hebrew newspaper in the country was printed in Tel Aviv. The Histadrut Labor Federation was quartered there as were the national offices for the Kupat Holim health plan. Jerusalem may have been a good place to relax spiritually, but all the excitement and vivacity of life in the tempestuous new country centered on the beach-front city that had been founded by Dizengoff and his band of pioneer adventurers.

In those days tourism was a synonym for Tel Aviv and Israeli nightlife was a euphemism for Dizengoff Street. Gourmet eating went on in the far northern precincts of the city where an alternate harbor had once been tried and where the cuisine ranged wide. There were more movie houses along a couple of Tel Aviv streets than in the entire city of Jerusalem and nearly all the country's discos and bars were only an amble away from the hotel strip on Hayarkon Street. Even Lod International Airport was another way of saying "Tel Aviv". Then something happened which changed Israel totally and irrevocably. It was called the Six-Day War, and it broke out on June 6, 1967.

The period immediately preceding the outbreak of war was one of the most tense in Israel's history. Egyptian President Gamel Abdul Nasser was sponsoring a *jihad* which threatened to erase the young Jewish state once and for all. To demonstrate his seriousness, Eilat was blockaded and Israeli shipping proscribed from the Red Sea. El Al flights destined for Kenya and South Africa were warned away from their traditional southern routes while Syria prepared to amputate the Galilee from the rest of Israel. All the Arab nations rushed volunteers into the region for what they saw as the decisive and ultimate battle.

When the smoke of war evaporated six days later, a completely different picture emerged. Israel was not only intact and relatively undamaged, but three and a half times larger than it had been in May. Suddenly, there was a whole buffer — Sinai — between Egypt and Israel. The Galilee was not only still Israeli; so were

the entire Golan Heights. Judea and Samaria were miraculously under Jewish rule again for the first time in 2000 years and, perhaps most significant, Jerusalem was reunited. The Western Wall was redeemed. The Old City was an integral part of Israel after its dismemberment in 1948. The national euphoria was unimaginable.

There was, however, a subtle message for Tel Aviv out of all this that was hard to discern at the time. Jerusalem was no longer a divided city with its most interesting artifacts and reminders of history partitioned away by barbed wire. No less than in the times of David and Solomon, it was the heart of the country. Most government offices were transferred to the capital. New immigrants were enticed to the hills. Industries were lured to the heartland of the country.

Israel underwent yet another cataclysm in 1973, when war broke out in October, on Yom Kippur. Again Israel emerged intact and victorious, but this time a heavy price had been extracted. The tremendous number of casualties was numbing. The cost of survival had not only paralyzed the economy, but had seriously mortgaged the future. Fewer people were coming into the country while more and more young Israelis were opting out. Labor disputes were also taking their toll, with hardly a month elapsing without some new disruption.

"The situation was difficult throughout the whole country, but I think it was even more difficult in Tel Aviv," explained a municipal official. "We had the same problems of everywhere else — and a few exclusively of our own as well. Young couples, for example, were not settling in the city, but heading to the suburbs. Tourism was hurting throughout Israel, but Tel Aviv had yet another problem — most of the travellers who were still coming were destined for Jerusalem and so the duration of their stays in Tel Aviv-Jaffa was drastically reduced.

"It seemed that we were losing on all fronts. Our population was growing older while young Tel Avivians fled elsewhere. The most important business interest in the city was badly damaged and it was questionable who and what would survive. The diamond industry was affected as well. And, at the same time, municipal appropriations from the government were being

CHANGING FACES OF TEL AVIV-JAFFA
The old and new meet easily in this city (above). In South Tel Aviv new buildings, such as Asia House (bottom right), spring skywards.

steadily reduced in consequence of a stagnant national economy. No one was sure what would happen."

What did happen in the 1980s was that a determined city administration and charismatic mayor took stock of the overall situation. Young families were provided with special incentives to stay in the city. These included more accessible mortgages, playgrounds and childcare centers. The entire tourist strip running adjacent to the beach was expanded and made more attractive. More attention was paid to public relations and advertising and a keener scrutiny was demanded of all tourist functions. Tel Aviv's beautiful and luxuriant Hayarkon Park became a center for summer events with free concerts featuring some of the world's top musicians. To counteract automotive and parking congestion in the city, the infamous "Denver Boots" were introduced, as well as special area parking tags for residents and foreign visitors.

At the same time, the splendid new highway connecting Tel Aviv with Ben-Gurion International Airport and Jerusalem was extended a few precious kilometers more, so that most of Tel Aviv's congested areas could be avoided completely. This meant that time to the airport was cut in half — and the 60 kilometers separating the country's commercial center with its capital were now negotiable in 45 minutes of non-speeding travel.

Lodz-born David Weisserman spent 62 of his 73 years in Tel Aviv. Widowed, retired and as irrepressible as his adopted city, he explained that his problem was

"We took a good Swiss idea and added the Israeli touch."

The word that best describes the spirit of Israel is dedication. In making the desert bloom, creating high-tech industries or developing international banking — dedication was behind each success.

And Bank Hapoalim, Israel's largest bank, truly reflects that spirit. One result is professional, dedicated Private Banking worldwide, with personalized confidential service.

Bank Hapoalim has a range of profitable investment instruments to offer our overseas clients including tax-free foreign currency accounts in Israel. Through our overseas banking network, we offer in-depth investment counselling covering various forms of asset management such as: deposit accounts, foreign exchange, bonds,

shares, precious metals and more. We also make available to our clients mutual funds managed by Fidelity Investments in the U.S. and G.T. Unit Managers Ltd. in the U.K. And our global communications network permits us to be all over the world at once.

With over $27 billion in assets, Bank Hapoalim has the strength and know-how needed in today's complex financial world.

Call us: Tel Aviv 972-32-243311
New York 1-212-830-5055, Zurich 41-209-7111, Luxembourg 352-475256, we'll provide you with information about Private Banking with the Israeli touch.

KESHER BAREL

Bank Hapoalim B M
A leading bank in size. And ideas.

Head Office: 50 Rothschild Blvd., 65124 Tel Aviv, Israel. Tel: (03)673333.
Regional Management - USA: 75 Rockefeller Plaza, 5th floor, New York, N.Y. 10019. Tel: (212)830-2800
Overseas Offices: Rockefeller Center, New York* • Plaza Branch, New York • Queens Branch , New York* • Huntington, New York*
Miami, Florida • Boston, Massachusetts* • Los Angeles, California* • Encino, California* • San Francisco, California*
Chicago, Illinois* • Philadelphia, Pennsylvania* • London, West End, England • London, City, England • Manchester, England
Zurich, Switzerland • Luxembourg • Georgetown, Grand Cayman • Toronto, Canada • Montreal, Canada
Buenos Aires, Argentina • Sao Paulo, Brazil • Rio de Janeiro, Brazil • Caracas, Venezuela • Punta del Este, Uruguay
Montevideo, Uruguay • Santiago, Chile • Panama City, Panama • Mexico City, Mexico
And 320 branches of the group in Israel   *Member F.D.I.C.

CHANGING FACES OF TEL AVIV-JAFFA
The city is not only people and architecture: it is windows and shutters too.

time. "Not time, God forbid, in the sense that I am afraid of dying. I decided a long time ago that I am an immortal. I mean that I don't have enough hours to do what I want — which is to swim summer and winter, play backgammon every afternoon, visit children, grandchildren and friends, go to the museums, walk in the parks, drink coffee in the cafés. Tel Aviv has almost too much for an old man.

"But now let me tell you something about this city of mine. People say that it is too crowded. I say that's good because the crowds are Jews and visitors and I love them both. People complain that there are too many cars in Tel Aviv so I tell them to go to Albania where they can cross the street more easily. They say that Tel Avivians are less patient than Jerusalemites and I agree absolutely because in Jerusalem nobody does anything but pray and make new income tax regulations. They say that Tel Aviv could be cleaner, so I point out that there is a rubbish bin on almost every street and why don't they use it? They say that Tel Aviv has too much concrete and is not as well planned as the capital and I ask them if they ever lived in a tent the way I did. They say that Tel Aviv is a crazy city and I say 'sure'. You got to be crazy to be a Jew. You got to be crazy to live in Israel. So why shouldn't the first Jewish city in the world be just a little bit fruitcake also?" □

29

Jaffa is one of the world's ancient cities
and the birthplace of many different
folk-tales. *Shlomo Shva* recounts its long
and rich history.

Legendary
Jaffa

A FAMOUS Greek legend was born on Jaffa's coast: the rescue of Andromeda by Perseus. According to the story, the sea god was angry with the people of Jaffa and sent a monster to destroy the city unless Andromeda, the king of Jaffa's daughter, was sacrificed to him. So the inhabitants of Jaffa tied Andromeda to a big rock in the sea and the monster was about to devour her when the hero, Perseus, came winging over the Jaffa skies. He saw Andromeda's peril, landed at once, slew the creature with his sword and saved the princess's life. The two young people fell in love and set off for Greece, where they lived happily ever after. When they died, the gods buried them among the stars, where they shine to this day. In Jaffa you can still see the rock where Andromeda was reputedly bound.

An old Egyptian legend also originates from Jaffa: King Thutmose III sent the commander of the Egyptian armed forces, Djehuti, to conquer Jaffa. Failing, Djehuti resorted to ruse. He sent a message to the governor of the city saying that he was so consumed with admiration for his bravery that he had decided to return to his own country. But first, as a measure of his esteem, he wished to entertain his rival at a festive banquet and confer a number of gifts on him and the people of Jaffa. Then Djehuti ordered soldiers to be hidden in the large baskets which were carried into the city. The moment the bearers passed through the city gates, the armed soldiers jumped out of the baskets and took Jaffa. This may be the first version of the famous story, *Ali Baba and the Forty Thieves.*

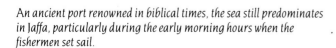

An ancient port renowned in biblical times, the sea still predominates in Jaffa, particularly during the early morning hours when the fishermen set sail.

As we read in the Bible, Jaffa was the port where King Solomon's sailors docked with the cedars of Lebanon they brought to build the splendid Temple in Jerusalem. It was also from Jaffa that the prophet Jonah left when he tried to escape the voice of God commanding him to go out to Nineveh and call the people there from their evil ways to righteousness. Jonah was subsequently swallowed by the Leviathan.

But Jaffa is not only a city of legends. Formerly, it was Jerusalem's harbor and the most important port during the Hasmonean and Second Temple periods. Fierce battles took place there between Jewish rebels and the Romans during the Great Rebellion of 67 CE. Peter, one of Jesus's first disciples, left from Jaffa to spread Christianity. And in Jaffa, Peter wrought a miracle: he restored to life Tabitha, whose burial place is still to be seen in eastern Jaffa in the courtyard of the Russian Orthodox church.

In the early centuries of the Christian era, Jaffa was bustling with activity and a large Jewish community settled there. The remains of an enormous cemetery have been found, where Jews from both Eretz Israel and distant places abroad were brought for burial.

Jaffa is associated with a number of famous monarchs. Richard the Lionheart, the English king who conquered Jaffa from the Moslems during the Crusades in 1191, fought fierce battles against the Egyptian ruler Salah e-Din and eventually signed a peace agreement with him. In 1228, King Friedrich II stayed there and strengthened Jaffa's fortifications. In 1250, another king arrived: Louis of France, known as Saint-Louis, who established a monastery. In the grounds of the Franciscan church, there still stands a statue of King Louis. Another great ruler came to Eretz Israel in 1799 after subduing Egypt. Napoleon besieged Jaffa and succeeded in taking it, but a terrible epidemic then struck his men. The story has it that Napoleon visited his soldiers in hospital, despite the risk of infection, so as to personally encourage them and boost their morale. This famous visit was commemorated in a painting, now hanging in the Louvre, and the Armenian monastery in Jaffa still displays the hall where the French emperor came to comfort his troops.

During this entire time, Jaffa served as a port of arrival for the hordes of pilgrims who streamed to Jerusalem. They would spend their first night lodged in the various monasteries of Jaffa. But the harbor was not deep enough for ships to come close, so they would anchor off the craggy coast and the passengers would be brought ashore in little boats making a perilous way between the rocks.

At the beginning of the nineteenth century, the city was destroyed and rebuilt: some 5000 inhabitants were concentrated on the hill overlooking the sea which was surrounded by a wall. In the 1830s the North African Jewish community began to establish itself and soon grew. In 1870, the first Eretz Israel agricultural school was founded near Jaffa in Mikve Israel and, soon afterwards, came the first agricultural colonies of the

The clocktower is one of Jaffa's most famous landmarks.

One can buy almost anything in Jaffa flea market — from copperware to mustard seeds and second-hand clothes.

Zionist renaissance. Jaffa became once more a center of Jewish settlement. The city grew, the walls came down and new neighborhoods, together with commercial enterprises, were built beyond the old boundaries. The harbor also intensified its activity as the country's central port. Towards the end of the century, the Jews built two new neighborhoods next to Jaffa: Neve Tsedek and Neve Shalom, today both centers of culture, art and theater.

Thousands of immigrant families from Bulgaria, Rumania and North Africa settled in Jaffa and opened shops, businesses and factories after the War of Independence and the Unification of Jaffa with Tel Aviv. The city took on a new face as a great deal of development began. A large park was built on the slopes from the hill to the sea. The old part of the city was rebuilt and now serves as an artists' quarter with galleries, boutiques, coffee-houses and entertainment spots all in special architectural surroundings. The old city, looking down on the scene of all the legends, attracts hundreds of visitors every night — both tourists and local people. Jaffa has picturesque restaurants and coffee bars that sparkle in the bright light, while after dusk the nightclubs and little theaters offer a variety of shows. Each of the many churches has its own tale to tell; every mosque has a history of wise or foolish rulers, of good or bad days gone by. There are old cemeteries, ruins of citadels and walls, sites of the royal battles of preceding generations.

At the heart of Jaffa stands the clocktower, built in honor of the birthday of a Turkish sultan. Nearby is the Turkish prison and the Flea Market well known to Israelis and tourists: on every corner and in every street, there is eager buying and selling of bargains, antiques, goods of all kinds perhaps no longer available in other shops. You hear the raucous cries of the market peddlers mingled with the customers arguing over the price: this is the din of bargaining which has filled this ancient city for thousands of years, since the times of the Kings of Judah and the Sages of the Talmud and the Mishnah, since the days of Jesus, the Crusaders, the Turks and the Mamelukes. The sounds of the past meet those of the present to form the voice of an old-new city. ☐

Shlomo Shva is an Israeli journalist who enjoys writing about Jaffa. His articles have been widely published in Israel and abroad.

33

Dizengoff is a concept

Let *Ruth Bondy*, **one of Israel's foremost journalists, take you on a wry and informative tour of Dizengoff Street. There, as you stroll from one end to the other, you will find Tel Aviv in microcosm.**

Right: Dizengoff is fashion, people and cafés.
Top: Carnival on Dizengoff Street.

DIZENGOFF Street begins far away. As it bears the name of the first mayor of Tel Aviv, semantically its roots are in Russia where he was born. Its topographic roots are German, for Dizengoff originates at the outskirts of what used to be Sarona, the site of a settlement of German Templars who came to Palestine in the second half of the nineteenth century to await the coming of the Messiah.

Today the area is known as Ha Kirya, and many government offices and public institutions are located there. Tel Aviv, the small garden suburb of Meir Dizengoff, became a large city, but his street remains at its center. Israelis, who are always in a hurry, don't waste their time on the word "street". They say, "Let's go to Dizengoff," "The entrance is on Allenby," "They live on Einstein." Dizengoff is more than a street name. It's also a concept which, according to one's age, beliefs and way of life, can imply *la dolce vita* — loafing bohemianism, hedonism or consumerism.

Nobody could say that Dizengoff is an elegant street. It is neither architecturally beautiful nor well planned. The most that can be said for it is that it's long, and that anyone who tried to eat their way through — from the *bourekas* at the corner of Ibn Gavirol to the *terrine de foie gras à la Strasbourg* at the northern end — without missing any of its dozens of cafés, kiosks, restaurants, pizzerias and ice cream parlors, would at best end up in the hospital. *Panta rhei*, the Greek phrase meaning "everything flows", is a good description of Dizengoff's eating places. It applies not only to the stream of customers, or even to the *tehina* dripping from the *pita*: the establishments themselves are in constant flux. The owners change, the names change, the chefs change. Overnight a Chinese restaurant becomes a French restaurant or vice-versa, depending on the latest gastronomic fashion. There were the falafel days, then the pizza period. The standard of living rose and it was steaks. The cost of food rose and steaks turned to hamburgers. Today we are in the great age of blintzes, stuffed with spinach, cheese or eggplant for a main course — and sweet ones for dessert.

Dizengoff has its spiritual assets as well. At one end are the Mann Auditorium, Habima (the national theater), and the Helena Rubinstein Pavilion, a wing of the Tel Aviv museum. In the middle we find the Cameri Theater and several cinemas. And at the far end there is a synagogue.

In some sections Dizengoff has all the appearance of a real city boulevard; elsewhere it's more like a small street in a Jewish *stetl*. There you find the shoemaker, the glazier, the locksmith *cum* repairman whose yard is a huge heap of iron scraps, craftsmen in blue undershirts, small shops selling hats and sewing accessories and dusty grocery stores where you can still buy on credit. These shops are never without their queues of basket-bearing housewives wearing dresses; nowadays only middle-aged women or older wear dresses on Dizengoff. The younger ones are clad according to fashion's latest dictates. They appear in running shorts, mini-togas, overalls, harem pants, jeans and tube tops — in short, anything which covers a little and reveals a lot.

The Dizengoff Building named after the city's first mayor, seen on the left from Dizengoff Square.

The houses, if anyone can be bothered looking at them, are mostly two or three stories high and boxlike. Many suffer from peeling plaster which, mercifully, is generally concealed by the trees. But who stares at housefronts needing paint when they can look at freshly painted young faces, plus all that comes with them, from bosom to ankle? Ah, the young beauties of Dizengoff!

Even the hardiest feet would not care to stroll the whole length of Dizengoff Street. So the site of the action, the locus of all appointments, scene of the Friday afternoon see and be seen, and headquarters for news of Friday night parties and diverse other pleasures, is to be found on the west side of the street from Dizengoff Circle — which faintly resembles a piazza with its water fountain and concrete benches — to, at most, the corner of Alozoroff. The east side has been "out" for many years, but its reputation is slowly growing again. Perhaps this is because on the other side the famous, old Cafe Rowal — once the Diamond Center of social engagements — has closed, and the status of Kassit, formerly home from home for the muses, has dropped. There in Kassit sat the greatest poets of the young Jewish state — the actors, and the best painters, many of whom left works on the walls in lieu of paying their bills. Today in the age of television, apparently even the muses spend their evenings watching *Dallas*. Dizengoff, like Jewish humor, is always found lacking when compared to the past.

Some of the prestigious shops have moved to new locations in north Tel Aviv, but there are still enough dress shops and shoe stores left to wear out any window shopper. Most of all there are boutiques. In Israel the word "boutique" doesn't necessarily mean that clothes are sold inside; it might as well be dogs, books, cheeses or olives.

After many years of stubborn insistence, both on the primacy of Hebrew over the dozens of tongues the Israelis brought with them when they returned to Zion, and on strict puritanism in language, the revolution has come. Many establishments have English names — "Bag", "Mash", "Honest", "American Dream" — perhaps as a sign of status. The guardians of the Hebrew language wanted to name the new shopping mall Lev Dizengoff (Heart of Dizengoff) but, to their dismay, they lost the battle. Elegant Dizengoff Center is an attempt to take the shopping-addicted Israeli off the streets and into shaded arcades. Up to now it has had only partial success. It seems as if, notwithstanding noise, sun, dust, and air pollution, the Israelis prefer the street. Perhaps they are afraid that something exciting might happen outside in their absence: a noisy debate between two cabdrivers over a scraped fender, or one of Israel's basketball stars might pass by — or an exceptionally exotic specimen of Dizengoff beauty.

The street is always pulsating, from early morning as working people arrive — in Israel, the workday starts early, seven or eight at the latest — until the last nightbird straggles home. Between them flow wave after wave of people from small towns out for a day of shopping in the big city, housewives snatching a couple hours of freedom while the children are in school, soldiers on temporary leave and loafers on permanent leave, quick snackers and leisurely lunchers, tourists staring at the ongoing parade, bands of noisy kids, elderly playboys on the hunt, proud fathers out for a stroll with their progeny, crowds exiting from a movie or theater — a moveable feat without end. And yet at dawn, you can hear the birds sing even on Dizengoff. □

Ruth Bondy has written a number of important books which have appeared in Israel, the USA and Europe. She has written for the Hebrew newspaper Davar *for many years.*

We were born together.

And we've thrived together ever since.

The Kaete Dan. Our first hotel. And as Israel grew, so did the Dan Hotels. Our friends came to stay again and again. More guests joined them. And so we opened more and more hotels. In the big cities where the action was. Beautiful resort hotels. And luxury budget hotels. That's how we became the biggest hotel chain in Israel.

This year, together with the State of Israel, we are celebrating 40 years. And what a celebration it's going to be!

Join us. You'll thrive on Dan hospitality.

40 THE DANS

ISRAEL AND THE DAN HOTELS
מדינת ישראל ומלונות דן

| Dan Panorama Tel Aviv | Dan Accadia Herzliya | Dan Tel Aviv | King David Jerusalem | Dan Carmel Haifa | Dan Caesarea | Dan Panorama Haifa |

Reaching for the stars

More than a million tourists choose Tel Aviv's splendid hotels each year, according to travel writer *Jordan Roberts*.

SOME Tel Aviv hoteliers rile when their city is called "Miami Beach on the Mediterranean". Others revel in the comparison. "Why not?" says one. "We have great luxury hotels fronting on miles of beach; as much sunshine as Florida — more even — and the best delicatessen in the Middle East . . . so what's so bad?"

Not much, according to the overwhelming majority of the one-million-plus tourists who stay at Tel Aviv hotels each year. And here, not unlike that place in Florida, the accent is definitely on luxury. More than half of this city-by-the-sea's 6000 hotel rooms are in the five-star luxury category.

The Dan, the *doyenne* of five-star hotels in Tel Aviv, has even instituted a private butler service in its newly completed top-class King David Wing. The butler will pack or unpack for you, lay out clothes, brush a suit, iron a cummerbund, polish shoes and take on whatever other Jeeves-like activities you require.

The genreral managers of five-star hotels everywhere often fancy their hostelries to be works of art, but in the case of the 300-room Dan Tel Aviv, it's a fact. In 1987, the hotel's facade was redesigned by the world-famous Israeli artist, Yaacov Agam, and the giant varicolored concrete-and-glass canvas can be seen and admired from as far as five miles away. The Dan is also deservedly famous for its Grill Room, which has long been a favorite with Israel's political and business elite.

Dan Hotels — the largest Israeli chain of five-star properties — recently added the 18-storey, 500-room Panorama to its list of acquisitions. It's the only major Tel Aviv hostelry to stand outside the serried rank of luxury hotels along Hayarkon Street.

The Panorama has the distinction of being the first top-class hotel in the city with easy access to historical Jaffa, with its splendid archeological treasures, excellent shopping, its wide array of *haute cuisine* and ethnic restaurants, and spate of nightclubs that entice visitors with everything ranging from Israeli folklore to some pretty daring "exotic" shows. It's also next to Tel Aviv's modern, seaside business center, and across the

Left: Tel Aviv beachfront along Hayarkon Street.

39

Above: Tel Aviv-Jaffa is one long, magnificent beach — splendid for surfing but offering protected swimming too.

Left: Overlooking the beach and close to most of the major hotels, the Kikar Atarim center contains restaurants and eateries to satisfy every palate and pocket book.

street from one of the city's prettiest parks (Charles Clore Park) and its most attractive beaches.

Israel's largest hotel — with over 600 rooms — is the Tel Aviv Hilton. The hotel is bounded on three sides by the trim lawns, subtropical trees and flowers of Independence Park. The fourth side fronts on the Mediterranean.

Constantly passing through its lobby is a veritable *Who's Who* of personalities — domestic and international — in politics, diplomacy, business and the arts. Many of them are whizzed up to one of the Hilton's top four Executive Floors that offer an array of elegant rooms and suites with extra touches of luxury.

Some of the suites run as high as $500 a day (including a morning newspaper), but to the rich and famous that's certainly no obstacle: Elizabeth Taylor, on her last visit, took an entire executive floor for herself and her entourage.

To make its executive accommodations even more exclusive, the Tel Aviv Hilton is planning to build an outside elevator to whisk its guests nonstop to the special floors and to the handsomely-appointed Executive Floors' check-in and lounge areas.

The Hilton's fashionable *King Solomon Grill* has a number of culinary firsts to its credit, but perhaps the most outstanding is its introduction of mullard to *haute cuisine*. The mullard is a high-class Israeli hybrid — a cross between a wild Muscovy duck and a domesticated Peking duck. The result is a remarkable fowl whose delicious meat tastes like the most tender beef. Naturally, it's expensive, but well worth the experience.

The Sheraton was the first international hotel chain to venture to Israel and its very high percentage of repeat business attests to its exacting standards and singular level of personal service. It has also devoted its top four floors — known as the Sheraton Towers — to executive and VIP rooms and suites. These have a separate check-in, and a thick-carpeted lounge where coffee, tea or milk . . . or champagne are served *gratis*.

Although the 350-room Sheraton has an array of restaurants befitting its five-star status, its culinary showcase is the exclusive, 56-seat *Twelve Tribes Grill Room*. Appetizers include a salad of fresh-caught Sea Bass with three dressings, and Carpaccio Pigeon, which is marinated breast of pigeon with basil and olive oil, served on a bed of red lettuce.

A third delectable favorite among gourmets is the Hot Paté of Goose Liver (Israel is, in fact, a major exporter of goose liver to *France*). In the entrée division, guests dote on Filet of Beef glazed with rosemary, mustard and bread crumbs. Aficionados of fish usually opt for the Farida — a splendid variety of Mediterranean Red Snapper — with avocado sauce. And if all these culinary delights weren't heady enough, one of the Sheraton's chef's dessert specialities is Iced Chivas Soufflé with fresh Fruit in Drambuie Sauce.

Postprandial activities at the Sheraton center around *Reflections* 2000 — the hotel's ever-popular disco. With state-of-the-art light and sound equipment and a seating and dancing capacity of 400, the disco throbs nightly halfway to dawn.

The Carlton, with its 282 rooms, is the smallest of the five-stars and therefore probably the coziest. But luxurious it most certainly is, and such stars as Brooke Shields, Grace Jones and Horst Buchholz have been recent guests. A stunning feature of the hotel is the rooftop pool, restaurant and the sun deck. From 15 storeys up, the panoramic views of the sea, the burgeoning city and the Judean Hills are breathtaking. On the more down-to-earth level, the Carlton's grill room, *The Silver Platter*, offers such terrestrial specialties as prime ribs, thick steaks and, on a more rarefied plane, Beef Bourguignon and spiced roast duckling.

Between the Carlton and the five-star Moriah Plaza on Hayarkon Street is the multistorey Kikar Atarim complex, which has dozens of mostly tourist-oriented shops, restaurants, bars and one of Tel Aviv's largest movie theaters, the Shahaf, that always seems to be showing the latest Woody Allen films.

The 18-storey Plaza was acquired not long ago by the Moriah chain of hotels, which is owned by Bank Hapoalim, Israel's largest bank. Seventy of its 350 rooms are on three executive floors. Recently added to the Plaza's facilities is a new seaview bar and a delicatessen restaurant. In addition to the pool, the hotel has direct access to the heart of Tel Aviv's lively beachfront.

Just down Hayarkon Street, within a shadow's reach of the Plaza, is the 300-room, 22-storey Diplomat Hotel, which is earmarked for some major improvements and refurbishing.

Next to the Diplomat, the Ramada Continental, peaking at 16 storeys, had 330 rooms plus an entire floor of suites. It boasts being the only Tel Aviv hotel with an indoor swimming pool — a pool with a view, at that: the swimming area has picture windows looking out on the beach and the Mediterranean, just yards away. The Ramada has a separate sundeck for lounging and tanning. In 1988 the hotel will be opening a new, enlarged health and fitness club all of whose facilities can be used by guests without extra charge. Also new for 1988 will be a poolside jacuzzi.

In addition to visiting statesmen, Tel Aviv's luxury hostelries regularly attract top personalities in the worlds of art, entertainment, theater, film and finance. Recent guests include Lauren Bacall, Placido Domingo (who started his carrer at the Tel Aviv Opera House), Goldie Hawn, Enrico Macias, Peter Ustinov, Shirley Bassey, Sean Connery, Tina Turner, Sylvester Stallone, Chuck Norris, John Hurt, Armand Hammer, Lee Marvin, Susan Strasberg, Leonard Cohen, Ray Charles, Bob Dylan, Samantha Fox, Hanna Schygulla, Lainie Kazan, Zubin Mehta, Shelley Winters and Diane Keaton. During their stay they were served kosher food; all Tel

Aviv's five-star hotels are kosher and some even offer *glatt* kosher fare, which adheres to the most exacting standards of the Jewish dietary laws.

At the time of writing, rates at the five-stars range from $55 a night for a single room to a high of $142 a night for a double. Suites are from $150 to $500. These prices can and do change, however, for all hotel categories.

One of the royal pleasures of the top-grade hotels is the Israeli Breakfast. Ironically, it was born in Israel's proletarian *kibbutzim* — the collective farm settlements — to stoke up farmers and farm hands for the long day of work ahead. The breakfast began with a variety of simple elements: tomato, cucumber, cottage cheese, a low-fat cream-type cheese, a nondescript yellow cheese, eggs, bread, butter or margarine, yoghurt, coffee or tea. The original plebian fare has undergone enormous changes in the last half-century — even in the *kibbutzim* — but there's no argument that the five-stars have elevated the Israeli Breakfast to its most delectable — some would say baroque — level.

Take, for instance, the Israeli Breakfast served at the Tel Aviv Hilton: Jaffa orange and Jaffa grapefruit juice; five varieties of cereal, including muesli, granola and oatmeal; cream cheese, smoked cheese, feta, camembert, brie, *chevre* (liberally sprinkled with poppy seed, sesame, onion or garlic), blue cheese, Swiss, cottage cheese, butter cheese and white cheese with dill and paprika (all from select Israeli dairies); olives, cucumbers, tomatoes, red peppers; boiled eggs, scrambled

eggs, fried eggs, egg salad; yoghurt, *lebeneh* (something between buttermilk and sour cream), sour cream; waffles, pancakes, French toast; herring in wine sauce, rollmops, smoked herring, herring in cream sauce, sea lox, *lakerda* and sprats; a variety of jams, marmalades and honey; apricot, pineapple and peach compote, applesauce and marinated figs; five kinds of cakes and pastries plus *halvah*. It's all sluiced down with unlimited quantities of freshly-brewed coffee or tea. This vast array of breakfast fare is laid out on a huge and beautifully decorated groaning board for you to come back to again and again for refills until you burst!

The Israeli Breakfast at the five-stars usually costs around $10, though the Dan Tel Aviv and Panorama include it *gratis* with the price of the room. Seven out of the nine four-star hotels in Tel Aviv also provide guests with an Israeli breakfast (albeit a somewhat more modest one) without extra charge.

Three of them — the Astor, Park and Concord — stand on the same seaside rank on Hayarkon Street as do the luxury hotels. Virtually across the street from them are the Basel, Grand Beach, Tal and Sinai. The Country Club and Ramat Aviv hotels are out of the city proper, but within the city limits. Both have expansive grounds and the 138-room Country Club has acres of sports facilities. The 118-room Ramat Aviv is nearer town, just over the Yarkon River, and close to the Haaretz Museum complex, Tel Aviv University, the Diaspora Museum and the Tel Aviv Fairgrounds. The two hotels are favored by long-stay guests, especially

families, as well as by overseas athletes and sports teams.

In town, the Basel Group has three hotels in the four-star category: the 138-room Basel, the 126-room Tal and the 92-room Concorde. The Basel has its own pool, but is, in any case, just across the street from the Gordon Pool, Tel Aviv's largest, sited right over the beach. It's also adjacent to the discos, shops and restaurants of Kikar Atarim.

The Tal hotel, sometimes known as the "Jolly Green Giant" because of its green-tiled facade, is a minute's walk from the beach and close to north Tel Aviv's lively nightlife. A drawing card for many long-stay guests is the fact that 27 of the hotel's rooms have kitchenettes.

The Concorde is at a vantage point on the seaside promenade and most of its rooms have a wide-angle view of the beach and the Mediterranean. The moderately-priced suites on its upper floors are much in demand. Out front, the sidewalk café-restaurant, Rowal, is a popular meeting place.

Less than a short walk back from the Concorde is Tel Aviv's largest four-star: the 260-room Sinai Hotel. The 16-storey Sinai boasts magnificent views of both the sea and the city; from the second-storey outdoor swimming pool and sun deck, guests can watch the passing parade on Tel Aviv's famed Ben Yehuda Street.

Standing 10 storeys high on Hayarkon Street between London Square and the US Embassy is the 100-room Park Hotel. The dining room — as do all the guest rooms — has a sea view. Its central location

makes it a popular place for business meetings and conferences.

The cozy (68-room) Astor Hotel is conveniently nestled between two five-star hotels — the Dan Tel Aviv and the Sheraton — on the sea side of Hayarkon Street. It recently came under new management, was completely refurbished and its previously dingy face transformed to a dazzling white. Two specialty restaurants — The Second Floor (fish and dairy) and The Panorama (meat) — established excellent reputations elsewhere in Tel Aviv before settling into their present location at the Astor. The restaurants have panoramic windows looking out to sea.

The Grand Beach is a few minutes' walk up Hayarkon Street from the Hilton. On the 10th floor, topping its 208 rooms, is the hotel's swimming pool and sundeck that afford splendid vistas in every direction. The hotel is especially mindful of the needs of Orthodox Jewish guests and boasts a synagogue, a "Sabbath elevator", "Sabbath clocks", and even special hours at the pool for men and women to bathe separately. One of the hotel's floors has been designated the Beach Club Floor, with superior appointments and such extra touches as an evening maid service, video films until midnight, and a minifridge.

The Marina Hotel in the Kikar Atarim Center has not been included in this rundown of four-star establishments, because — as in the case of the five-star Diplomat, which is under the same ownership — it is scheduled to change hands and may be closed for refurbishing during part of 1988.

The four-stars — like all the luxury hotels — have kosher cuisine. Rates per room vary from $35 to $90. The three-star hotels cluster close to their higher-class neighbors around Hayarkon Street like children peeking behind their mothers' skirts. Since the marked upswing in Israeli tourism at the end of 1986, many of the hotels in this category have been undergoing extensive renovations.

The largest among the three-stars is the highly commended 96-room City Hotel, which is a Basel Hotel Group property. Its convenient location close to the Sheraton and wonderful sea views from many of its rooms keep it full nearly all year around. Room rates at the three-stars are from $20 to $56.

Tel Aviv's dozen two-star and one-star hotels are mainly for the young, the young in heart, and rock-bottom budget travelers. Rates at these hostelries range from a low of $8.50 per room to, say, $40 at the two-star Armon Hayarkon — which has been revamped and is very well located. Note that all Tel Aviv hotels of *whatever* class that serve food and drink *must* be prepared to serve guests freshly-squeezed orange juice on request anytime during the country's long citrus season (October through May). In Israel — which is enormously proud of its world-famous Jaffa oranges — it's the law. □

Jordan Roberts has been a radio journalist in Israel for more than 20 years. He writes regularly for some of the world's leading travel publications.

נופש פעיל באמצעות -
מועדון ספורט הים האדום

RED SEA SPORTS CLUB

A Right
Royal Sports Club

The "Red Sea Sports Club" offers you more water-sports and desert adventures than any other sport club in Israel. The club is under highly professional and experienced management, including qualified instructors conversant in several languages. We will be happy to welcome you to our offices at the King's Wharf, by the lagoon next to King Solomon's Palace.

You can obtain further details from the reception desk at your hotel, from your travel agent, or by calling us direct 059-79111, 059-73725, 059-79685, 059-76569 We look forward to seeing you!

45

Israel's capital of culture

Tel Aviv-Jaffa is the cultural epicenter of Israel. Here *Jeremy Kitling* describes the vast range of theater, ballet, cinema and nightlife to be found in the country's most exciting city.

"HAIFA works, Jerusalem prays and Tel Aviv plays." This was already an old wheeze half a century ago — that is, even before the state of Israel came into being. On the whole, however, the formula pretty much still applies. Modern-day Tel Aviv *is* the cultural and entertainment capital of Israel. Long after they've rolled up the sidewalks in Haifa and Jersualem, Tel Aviv is still brimming with life and excitement.

The city's most famous cultural treasure is undoubtedly the world class Israel Philharmonic Orchestra. Less well known, but of extremely high professional caliber, is the Israel Chamber Orchestra, entering its 21st year in 1988. The orchestra, founded by conductor Gary Bertini, often features internationally-known soloists and performs most of its concerts in the handsome Recanati Hall of the Tel Aviv Museum.

Tel Avivians are also crazy about ballet, supporting no fewer than six ballet companies. Probably best known is the Batsheva group, who perform mainly modern ballet. Its one-time ballerina and choreo-

Habima (left) is not only home for Israel's national theater, but has played a central role in the revival of the Hebrew language. Habima is considered one of the world's best national repertory theaters.

47

grapher, Rina Schoenfeld, who has received rave reviews from dance critics around the world, recently formed her own dance company.

A mixture of modern and classical ballet is the provenance of the Bat Dor Company, while purely classical dance fills the repertoire of the relatively new, but up-and-coming Israel Ballet. The Inbal Dance Theater is a hardy perennial, delighting audiences for decades with its renditions of dance patterns drawn from the ancient Jewish community of Yemen. Its costumes — rich in exquisite detail — are often as fascinating as the rhythmic dances themselves. Israel's most experimental dance company is Moshe Ephrati's Kol U'dmamah (Sound and Silence) group, so called because many of his dancers are deaf, but can "hear" the music and rhythm through their bare feet as they touch the vibrating floorboards.

Israel's national theater — Habimah — came to Tel Aviv by way of Moscow, with the great Stanislavsky as its first mentor, and Berlin, when in the 1920s, it was a

Tel Aviv Auditorium.

hub of avant garde theater. Habimah settled here in 1931 and its shining star, Hanna Rovina, dominated the Israeli stage for the next 30 years. Rovina is to Israeli theater what Ethel Barrymore is to American, Mrs Siddons to English, and Sarah Bernhardt to French theater. Habimah is on Tarsat Boulevard next to the Mann Auditorium (home of the Israeli Philharmonic) and the Helena Rubinstein Pavilion of the Tel Aviv Museum. It still draws heavily on classical Hebrew repertoire with plays like The Dybbuk and The Golem, and contemporary Hebrew works. A lack of Hebrew shouldn't put you off paying a visit to this famed theater — earphones are available for simultaneous translation into English.

The Cameri Theater on Frishman Street, just off Dizengoff Street, is the country's second-largest theater. It focuses on modern — and frequently more controversial — Hebrew works, but also has Hebrew versions of Broadway and London hits. Last season's sellout was Les Miserables. Various smaller theaters scattered around the city sometimes put on plays in

English. The English-language daily Jerusalem Post has a regular listing of theatrical offerings in Tel Aviv, and the ThY '81 Studio at 1 Tveria Street is a pocket theater putting on three English-language presentations — from Chekhov to Beckett — each week.

There is an extraordinary number of museums in Tel Aviv and its environs. The Museum of Tel Aviv, for example, provides a distinguished and regular forum for lectures and slide presentations. Similarly, the Zionist Organization of America's ZOA House on Daniel Frish Street, near Ibn Gvirol Avenue, has Thursday night lectures and regular dramatic readings in English.

For those who prefer the peripatetic rather than the sedentary approach, Tel Aviv offers a wide variety of excellent organized tours which are usually free. These include Tel Aviv University and Bar Ilan, the Women's International Zionist Organization (WIZO), and Hadassah's Tourism Department.

Some truly fine summer evening concerts are held in Yarkon Park, which straddles the Yarkon River in north Tel Aviv. These presentations are first-rate and attract leading performers from all over the world. The park itself, covering 1200 acres and larger than Central Park in New York, is well worth a visit. Small steamers ply upstream for a few miles, huge eucalyptus trees shading part of the journey. The boats were originally painted white, bringing to mind a scene from The African Queen. There are also rowboats and paddleboats for rent by the hour.

In addition to a large sports area, which includes a big skateboard court, there's a huge tropical garden, a rose garden with over 700 varieties, a lake with sailing, windsurfing and rowing facilities, picnic areas, a cafe, a restaurant and a Disneyland-style mini-train that stops at various points in the park. Luna Park, an amusement park with a small roller coaster and other rides, lies next to the northern edge of the Yarkon Park as do the Tel Aviv Fair Grounds.

On the other side of town, in Old Jaffa, is Israel's longest-running hit, The Israel Experience — an hourlong, tearjerking multi-media spectacular showing the grand sweep of Israel past and present. A stereo soundtrack accompanies the picture on a giant, 67-ft screen, onto which multiple images are thrown by computer-coordinated projectors. The Israel Experience has been playing for several years and has been seen by more than half a million people. The special screening hall is at 4 Pasteur Street, near the entrance to the old port of Jaffa. Tickets cost approximately $5.

Tel Avivians are fanatical movie fans and 50 of Israel's 150 movie houses are within the city's precincts. These are popular because first-run films playing in New York or London are usually playing in Tel Aviv at the same time. They are not dubbed, but have sub-titles in two languages (usually English and French for Israeli, that is Hebrew-language, movies). There is also an excellent art cinema at the Museum of Tel Aviv.

Going to the movies is also a good way to get an inside glimpse of Israeli life. Feature films are usually prefaced by 15 minutes of advertisements for various

The Promenade Coffee Shop where concert and play-goers conclude the evening's programme.

Israeli products and services. Some are hilarious!

Famous not only for traditional cultural outlets, Tel Aviv is noted also for its nightspots which provide a different forum of musical emphasis. In fact, many Tel Avivians say it's only when the theaters empty that the town really starts rolling. Here is a random sample of nightspots where "the middle of the night is high noon."

Where Trumpeldor Street meets Ben-Yehuda, we find the Bonanza, a bar and restaurant with singers and other home-grown live entertainment. Russalka, a restaurant on the seaside promenade, features Russian singers along with the *blini* and chicken Kiev. Further down the promenade (Hebrew, *tayalet*), the Rock Cafe belts out Israeli rock 'n' roll. Nearby is Herbie Sams, a toney restaurant-disco. Above the Gordon Pool, next to Kikar Atarim, is the large, new La Diva — one of the latest trendy places for dining and disco dancing.

The Dixieland on Hayarkon Street, opposite the Tal Hotel, puts the accent on jazz. A 1930s-style dinner-dance restaurant is the Pilz, whose art-decor interior looks like something out of a Fred Astaire/Ginger Rogers movie: on Hayarkon between London Square and the Park Hotel.

The hottest spot in town on Dizengoff, called the Divine, is a bar-restaurant with singers. And the open-air Terminal Coffee house-restaurant at the corner of Gordon and Dizengoff is a favorite Yuppie hangout.

If you fancy a big disco, there is the circular Colosseum in Kikar Atarim. And on Yitzhak Sadeh and Giborei Yisrael Street, the Cinerama's heavy decibel count as a disco is easily matched by live sounds when it serves as a concert venue for Israeli, American and European pop and rock stars. The Trumpeldor, at the base of Trumpeldor Street opposite the Concorde Hotel, is a bar-restaurant with jazz and other live music. A few blocks down, near the Old Opera House, is the Amadeus — a favorite haunt of actors, painters, musicians who like to come after their last gig, and journalists and bohemians in general.

Practically every part of Old Jaffa is alive with entertainment till the early hours. There are ethnic restaurants with performers and bands, like the Greek Adriana; variety shows with strip acts can be seen at November, and popular singers and comedians feature at the Hamam and Omar Khayam nightclubs. Tel Aviv bon vivants will tell you that the best nights to go out are from Monday through Thursday. The nights *not* to go out are Friday and Saturday. Why? "That's when the hicks come to town." □

Jeremy Kitling originates from London and has written extensively about Israel for 15 years. While many of his articles deal with politics, he admits that ballet and theater interest him most.

In search of an Israeli cuisine

Tel Aviv offers an incredibly wide range of restaurants to suit almost any palate and pocketbook. One of Israel's most renowned authorities on the subject of food, *Suzy David,* provides background and hints.

The search for raw ingredients. Top: a pitta bakery in Jaffa. Above: cyclists in the Carmel Food Market.

Fresh falafel stands are never far away in Tel Aviv. This one is in the Bezalel Market.

WHAT is Israeli cuisine? Here are just a few of its constituents: Hungarian goulash, Rumanian *mititei*, Turkish doner kebab, Greek *tiropita*, Polish gefilte fish, Arab *medjaclara*, Yemenite *jahnun*, Iranian rice, Russian *blini*, Mexican *enchiladas*, Czechoslovakian *knoedel*, German *sauerbraten*. And then, of course, there are the tried and true *humus*, *tehina* and *falafel*. Israeli gastronomy is obviously still in flux — and in search of an ethnic identity. The various flavors, aromas and condiments being used are slowly being melded into new combinations and tastes which may one day produce a real national cuisine.

When I arrived in Israel over 40 years ago, Israeli cuisine was quite different from today's. Simple and uncluttered restaurants were mainly to be found around the lower part of the Herzl Street area, catering mainly to merchants, shopkeepers and workers as well as to the kitchenless newcomers who often tried unsuccessfully to match their imported tastes with what was available in the struggling new country. The food was simple, honest and good, leaning heavily on the food cultures of Turkey, Greece, and Bulgaria. Succulent stuffed aubergines, vine leaves, peppers, courgettes, spinach, meat or cheese pies were basic components. There was also good, thick bean soup, and yogurt soup was almost ubiquitous. Not too bad, I assure you. Food was cheap and so was everything else. Only money was expensive.

I used to eat at a place, long since disappeared, called Tnuva. It was one of many dairy restaurants that offered the most reasonable fare. Depending on the mood or savvy of the owner, who was usually more of a shopkeeper than a restaurateur, you could end up with superb pickled herring or a leathery omelet. Meals at Tnuva usually concluded with what was known as fruit soup — an item that disappeared from the gastronomical lexicon of Israel only to reappear, albeit paradoxically, on *nouvelle cuisine* menus in France. I don't think we Israelis can claim copyright, however!

When the Yemenite *aliya* arrived *en masse* in the late 1940s, the new immigrants settled in the southern part of the Carmel Market near Jaffa. Soon the Yemenites opened new restaurants serving their own brand of food that was greeted enthusiastically by an Israeli public used to bland tastes. It was another culinary milestone.

The Carmel Market is, incidentally, like almost all open markets I know, a joy to visit. It throbs with life, color and noise. It's a pity I can no longer acquire a kilo of shrimp for two lira (there were no takers at the time!), or have my fishmonger Leon offer me a tiny grilled *barbounia* and an *arak* to wash it down while waiting for him to energetically clean the other fish I bought. Things have changed, but the market is still a great place to visit.

With Rumanian, Yugoslavian and Bulgarian immigration Jaffa became the focal point for settlers. Restaurants began to mushroom and the choice of food widened even more. There were, and still are, rivalries: whose food is better? Are Rumanian *midites* tastier than Bulgarian *metvuzno kofte*? Whatever your verdict, you will certainly find they are very different.

The produce often arrives in the Carmel Food Market before the sun —fresh cucumbers, tomatoes and watermelons spilling off trucks and onto the stands adjacent to the Yemenite Quarters and near the old Tel Aviv-Jaffa border. The whole marketplace is rinsed in colours: a noisy, boisterous 'happening' that occurs every day of the week, except Saturdays and holidays, where thousands of Israelis converge in search of 'metsias' or bargains. What really counts most, however, is not price, but freshness.

The Arabs contributed with their excellent *tehina*, *humus* and *falafel* — and we became addicted to the stuff. Entertaining at home was informal; very often people would drop by and be invited to share a meal, or maybe just some olives and wine. When we were still newcomers to Israel, a bottle of wine cost a few piasters and was quite drinkable — but then perhaps my tastes were as yet no so refined and sharpened by the multitude of different brands of wine that have appeared on the market ever since.

Some of the restaurants around Herzl Street already mentioned have long since disappeared, but the few that remain are still quite good. In the 1960s and 1970s — notwithstanding wars and their aftermath — fancier restaurants started springing up. While there was, by then, a vast reservoir of culinary know-how in Israel, and while you could have the most exquisite meals in private houses, the food at large was rather non-committal.

I have a feeling that around this time there was a desire to invent an instant Israeli cuisine. Well, I don't think we're there yet. Not being immune to outside influences, however, we have plenty of pizzerias, hamburger stands, chicken in and out of the basket and, lately, a multitude of Chinese, Japanese, Indonesian and Indian restaurants.

The 1980s brought not only more fancy restaurants and exotic names on the menus, but also a new awareness of high quality food and its health aspects — with more attention paid toward its preparation and appearance. A new interest is being generated around cooking and this isn't an isolated phenomenon. Men are now increasingly taking more interest and are rolling up their shirt sleeves to relax in the kitchen after work before preparing the evening meal — something to be encouraged as much as possible by us women. In short, food has become fashionable.

Now, with the state of Israel reaching its 40th

All-night pitta bakery in Jaffa.

anniversary and Tel Aviv approaching almost twice that age, we are still learning about cookery. All the necessary ingredients for an honest, authentic Israeli cuisine are here: expertise, variety, fresh fruit and vegetables, fish, fowl — and much, much more. I invite you to be patient — and to enjoy the multiplicity of choices Tel Aviv has to offer. □

Suzy David was born in Bulgaria and has spent all her adult life in Tel Aviv. Her cookbooks are major bestsellers and she is considered one of the real authorities about food in Israel.

Café society

A tourist strolling down Tel Aviv's main shopping streets might get the impression that the entire city is on holiday. Everyone seems to be strolling around while the outdoor cafés dotting the pavement are brimming over with people.

Tel Avivians love going out; their favorite daytime activity is café-going — which is as much a part of Tel Aviv's way of life as working and eating. Most self-respecting Tel Avivians find themselves in a café at least once a day.

A café is the place to get the day off to a good start with a croissant and *café hafuch* — a steaming brew of strong coffee and hot milk. Business meetings take place in cafés over coffee and snacks. Cafés are where friends meet, interviews are held, and women meet to discuss the important issues of the day over whipped-cream-topped capuccino.

Part of the cafés' allure is pure snob appeal. Where

else can you hobnob with local film stars, pop singers and sports idols, or sit elbow to elbow with the top model you saw in a movie commercial the previous night? Meeting celebrities apart, café-going has become the main phenomenon of Tel Aviv's street culture. And Dizengoff, the city's most elegant thoroughfare, has a café culture all its own.

In Café Kassit, on Dizengoff, many of the country's literary and theatrical luminaries used to meet regularly; famous poets, such as Natan Alterman and Avraham Shlonsky, had regular tables reserved for them. Further north on the same street, Café Stern, now a fish restaurant, was the longtime haunt of self-styled refugees belonging to the Austro-Hungarian aristocracy, who would eat their strudel nowhere else. Impeccably coiffed Polish ladies are still seen every morning at Café Ugati and Afarsemon. More recent additions to Dizengoff's café scene are Le Croissant, which seems to attract a chic young crowd, and the Apropo and Habimah cafés. Cafés Frak, Pinati, Ditza, and Cherry are equally famous.

At no time are Dizengoff's cafés fuller or noisier than on Friday afternoons, when they act as magnets for the singles crowd to pick up partners of the opposite (or same, as the case may be) sex — and find out what good parties are on that night.

If you were to emulate a typical Tel Avivian's Friday afternoon, it would resemble something like this: get up late, have lunch at Habimah Café, the Sifriya or Café Batya; amble over to Kassit or Café Tamar, where pillars of the literary and bohemian community gather regularly. Then on to Bonanza, where many Kassit and other Dizengoff Café regulars have migrated in the past year or two. Other Tel Avivians spend the afternoon at what Israelis call the meat markets — pick-up joints — such as Cherry, or the Kum Kum, while the nouveau

Facing page:
No sleep for the young in Tel Aviv — dancing continues on the beach from midnight to dawn.

The second contribution to this book
by Michal Yudelman deals with one of
Tel Aviv's most cherished institutions,
the sidewalk café.

The Café Kassit has been a favourite haunt for intellectuals and the famous for many years.

riche crowd hangs out at Exodus and Olga, near the prestigious Kikar Hamedina shopping circus.

The city's rapidly increasing young population has had a strong influence on its social habits and entertainment. Consequently, the café-going trend has expanded to the evening and night hours. The social scene in Tel Aviv has become so vibrant, intense and hectic that many Tel Avivians seem never to sleep at all. In fact, people from other towns like to say that Tel Avivians walk around with their eyes closed during the day because they never sleep at night. The center of Israel's nightlife, entertainment and singles' scene, Tel Aviv is as fast-laned and cosmopolitan as any European capital, if not more so.

On Friday and Saturday nights, the city is invaded by so many out-of-towners that hard-pressed residents have started going out on Thursday nights instead. For the past couple of years, no Tel Avivian worth his salt would want to be seen dead in any public place on a weekend, reserving those nights for private parties and trips out of town.

As with the daytime cafés, every few weeks another new place emerges as the only place in town to be. Inevitably, these places fill up with groupies — so the hard-core patrons, whose exclusive club has been discovered, move on to the next fashionable haunt. This happened with the Red Bar, the Sifriya, the West Coast, Zela Bira, Shoftim, Takam, Arnold's and many others.

New places are never in short supply. They spring up almost overnight to accommodate the ever-growing crowds of late-night revellers. Ivgi, Downtown, Riviera, Bograshov Gallery, Rock Café, Next, Boursa, White House and Terminal are just a few of the haunts which have opened recently. And the Cinerama, the largest disco in the Middle East, packs in thousands of round-eyed youngsters and has a VIP club for the older, heavier and wealthier crowd who want to feel they're still with it.

On summer nights it's hard to tell whether it's the heat or the compulsion to socialize that sends thousands of young people down to the seaside promenade. The main attraction there seems to be a stark concrete square filled with rickety chairs and tables, whose specialty is watermelon with salty white cheese on the side. Appropriately, the place is known as Avatihim — Hebrew for watermelons — and is usually bursting at the seams with people. On Thursday night, just to hang around eyeing the lucky ones who made it to a table and survived counts for being there. Hundreds make do with this; they can still tell their friends when they meet for coffee the following afternoon, "Oh, I was at Avatihim last night." Other restaurants along the promenade hastened to follow suit and on Friday and Saturday nights it's impossible to find a vacant table.

Eventually, even Thursday nights were to become too crowded for the fickle Tel Avivian who began to look for ways of avoiding the masses and started going out on Wednesdays. Some clubs took to offering special programs on that night to cater to a larger crowd of clients. One night spot, for instance, Makom Bahutz (a place outside), on the Tel Baruch Beach north of Tel Aviv, opens on Wednesday nights only. Not that anyone ever went to check whether it was still there on Tuesday or Thursday — it's just that as far as Tel Aviv was concerned, it was only there on Wednesday. Other places became Tuesday places, Monday places and even Sunday places.

Today, Tel Aviv nights resemble one huge, never-ending celebration which everyone joins in without really knowing what it's all about — except that the party must go on. ☐

Michal Yudelman is a feature writer for the Jerusalem Post *and also works as an editor for* Metro, *a regional paper specializing in Tel Aviv.*

The sound of music

The Israel Philharmonic Orchestra has been playing to local and international audiences for more than 50 years. Music critic *Benjamin Toller* explains why the IPO has achieved such an outstanding reputation.

Above: Zubin Mehta conducts the Israel Philharmonic Orchestra.

THEY played in 1936 under the guest conductorship of Arturo Toscanini as a declaration of hope for the Jews of Palestine — and as a protest against the Nazi persecution of artists. In the early 1940s they played again for the volunteers of the Jewish Brigade, who were poised to stop Rommel's sweep across North Africa. Traveling along Israel's "Burma Road" in 1948 in hastily improvized tanks and armored personnel carriers, their music reached a Jerusalem nearly starved and bludgeoned into submission but still refusing to surrender. Appearing before the troops in every subsequent war, they filled the desert with Bach and Brahms while the prevailing background music was the sound of exploding shells and sniper exchanges. Twelve years older than the State of Israel and permanently housed in Tel Aviv's beautiful Mann Auditorium, the Israel Philharmonic Orchestra is one of the country's most extraordinary success stories.

Former child prodigy and internationally acclaimed Polish violinist Bronislaw Huberman already sensed in the early and mid-1930s that the Jews of central Europe were doomed. Hitler's anti-Semitism was taking its toll; Jews were being beaten, ostracized, and deprived of basic civil liberties. Already considered one of the world's most masterful violinists, Huberman could have found sanctuary and employment almost anywhere — but saw a much larger and grimmer picture than merely that which lay in store for him personally. European Jewry provided a disproportionate number of the finest musicians alive. What

would happen to them? Where would they go? How would they continue playing?

Huberman decided that the only satisfactory answer was Palestine and he convinced other leading musicians to cross the Mediterranean with him in search of a haven which would permit and not stifle artistic expression. By 1936, while Europe was moving inexorably toward war and destruction, the founding of the Palestine Symphony Orchestra was announced and Toscanini agreed to preside over the first concert in Tel Aviv, to take place in October.

The Tel Aviv-based orchestra was different for many reasons — not the least being its uniqueness in the Middle East, where ululations were far more prevalent than concertos. In particular, the refugee musicians were fiercely individualistic. Many were virtuosos and had to be handled accordingly, which frequently led to some friendly anarchy. Then there was the problem of communications. Some spoke Yiddish, others Hebrew, German, Polish or Russian. Since it seemed that no one conductor could contend with the obstreperousness of 115 adamant individualists who could cause both music and mayhem when squeezed together on a narrow stage, a roster system for the orchestra's conductors was adopted almost from the very beginning. Thus such musical luminaries as Bernstein, Koussevitsky, Munch, Monteux, Barbirolli, Mitropoulos and Ormandy alternately conducted the assemblage which became the Israel Philharmonic Orchestra in 1948 — first playing *Hatikva*, Israel's national anthem, as an accompaniment to David Ben-Gurion's reading of Israel's declaration of independence.

When the IPO began touring in the early 1950s it was viewed more as a curiosity than a musical reality. Israel itself was only vaguely etched into people's minds so what could one expect of its orchestra? Any doubts were dispelled quickly, however. Wherever the IPO was heard, in the United States or Europe, the acclaim was uniform. Israel not only had an orchestra, it had a superb one. But no orchestra lives on touring alone and the IPO was an instant success in Israel. Its 40 000 annual subscribers today represent the largest subscription audience in the world — a legacy spanning decades.

In 1961, Zubin Mehta appeared as guest conductor for the first time and the chemistry, as one of the musicians described, was excellent. The brilliant Indian-born musicologist was invited back to Tel Aviv frequently in the intervening years, presiding over one emotion-filled concert in Jerusalem just after the Six-Day War in 1967. He was appointed musical advisor in 1969, director in 1977 and director for life in 1981. Under Mehta's dynamic and careful supervision, the IPO developed distinctively and rapidly. A marriage between Bach and rock, for example, created a sensation, particularly among the younger generation of music lovers. Then the existing repertoire was expanded by introducing pre-Baroque selections under a special program called Musica Viva. But Mehta was not only an apostle of variety. He was also acutely aware of the changing demographics of a new state — in which oriental or eastern Jews already enjoyed numerical supremacy, and where the median age was getting younger all the time. So the IPO began appearing in public parks and university campuses, in Eilat and in the Roman amphitheatre in Caesarea. For many who knew nothing about western classical music before, exposure to Debussy and Stravinsky provided a bridge between dissimilar cultures. In all, the experiment was an astonishing success.

Interestingly, the role of the IPO as a refuge for musicians hasn't changed that much in the past 52 years. In fact, considering that a quarter of the IPO's members are of Russian origin, it is almost as if Huberman were still orchestrating. There are also quite a few Americans in the musical group, most of whom have sacrificed two-thirds of their former salaries for the privilege of playing with the IPO. Even with the prestige gained by belonging to the Israeli orchestra, life is not easy. There are long rehearsals every day, including Friday, in addition to concert schedules that would boggle musicians everywhere. There is plenty of travel during tours, but that too is not fun. On one memorable occasion, there were 19 separate appearances in 21 days.

Despite fame, success, over-subscription at home, and high over-sales abroad, the IPO is still far from profitable or even balanced. With or without money, however, the IPO is surely one of Israel's most precious resources. As one veteran musician explained: "We're not easy, but we're good. We don't only make music, we make friends. I think over the years we've performed more diplomacy than the Foreign Ministry. I guess that's what Huberman really wanted — a Jewish orchestra talking to the whole world." □

Benjamin Toller is an American music critic who has visited Israel on numerous occasions, and admits to being an outspoken admirer of the IPO.

The wonderful world of museums

Sculpture outside the Tel Aviv Museum.

There are so many excellent museums in and around Tel Aviv that a concerted effort is needed just to take in the main exhibitions, as described here **by** *Franz Asherman.*

ONLY when you consider that the entire municipal population of Tel Aviv-Jaffa — about a third of a million inhabitants without the suburbs — could be distilled in small sections of New York or London without even producing ripples, can you appreciate fully the real cultural achievement of the first, modern, Jewish metropolis.

In the realm of preserving and exhibiting objects of permanent importance to the arts and sciences Tel Aviv-Jaffa is second to none. There is never an interval without important art exhibitions, featuring both local and international talent, or photo displays, or the results of new excavations. Indeed, there are so many museum-related activities taking place simultaneously in Tel Aviv-Jaffa that it requires determination, dedication and stamina to take in just the main events.

The first Tel Aviv Museum was the home of the city's first mayor, Meir Dizengoff, and was opened to the public in 1932. It was actually in the hall of the museum that David Ben-Gurion proclaimed an independent state on May 15, 1948. Opened in 1971, the present museum on Shaul Hamelech Boulevard contains 1300 square meters of exhibition space, concert halls and auditoriums where paintings, sculpture, graphics, photography and design are regularly shown and where there are regular dance, theater and cinema events on most evenings. There is a permanent collection of fine Israeli paintings covering the period from prestate to the 1980s, but there is nothing parochial about the museum, which lures some of the world's finest art to Tel Aviv.

In addition to the main museum building, which is in an area eventually scheduled to become the cultural heart of the city, there is the Helena Rubenstein Pavilion near the Habima Theater, and the Thomas Mann Auditorium, which opened in 1959. Together, the complex hosts more than 600 000 visitors annually.

The museum is open from Sunday to Thursday between 10am and 2pm and from 5–9pm. Closed on Fridays, it is open on Saturday from 11am to 2pm and again from 7–10pm. The Pavilion is open Saturday morning hours only and closes two hours earlier during weekdays. More often than not, most Tel Aviv museums are free on Saturdays if they remain open on the Sabbath, and charge only nominal admission fees during the rest of the week.

The Tel Aviv Museum has its counterparts elsewhere in other major cities. This, however, cannot be said of the Nahum Goldmann Museum of the Jewish Diaspora (Beth Hatefusot), which is on the campus of Tel Aviv University in nearby Ramat Aviv. This unique edifice, which really should not be missed, concentrates on the evolution and history of Jewish communities the world over. Here, only a few minutes from central Tel Aviv, the latest audio-visual techniques are used to tell the story of the long and variegated history of the Jewish people. There is an exquisite model of a thirteenth-century community complete with more than one hundred tiny figurines, perfectly clad for the occasion. There are films and displays showing village life in East Europe, Greece and Morocco, and a Chinese synagogue rendition which retraces an almost forgotten moment of Jewish history over 300 years ago. For a paltry charge, you can get a computer printout of any one of 3000 Jewish communities which once existed and there is a taped dialogue between the thirteenth-century monk, Pablo Christiani and the Jewish scholar, Nachmanides, about whether or not Jesus was truly the messiah.

I have gone to this museum no less than a dozen times. I have taken every overseas guest who has ever visited me. When my children were taken there during school outings, I was gratified. It has no other counterpart in the world.

Again, the cost of admission is nominal, and free on Saturdays between the hours of 10am and 2pm. The museum is open on Sunday, Monday and Thursday from 10am to 5pm, and on Tuesday and Wednesday from 3–10pm.

Another cultural oasis just a tumble from North Tel Aviv over the Hayarkon Bridge is the Ha'aretz Museum Complex. This comprises a whole group of extremely interesting units covering a wide range of interest around an ancient site called Tel Qasile, where ancient Hebrew, Philistine and Roman artifacts were uncovered. Although the museums comprising the complex are not large, they range over a surprisingly wide spectrum.

For example, the Ha'aretz Museum of Ancient Glass (located in a circular, green building) specializes in the ancient glassware once indigenous to the region. Some of its carefully unearthed displays are considered unique. Then there is the Kadmon Numismatic Museum which concentrates on old coins from the region's various epochs. A new addition, the Alphabet Museum, shows the history and development of alphabets and writing in a graphic exhibition of the evolution of written communication, from the Semitic tongues to Greek and Latin. There is the Museum of Ethnography and Folklore, which concentrates on the customs and costumes of the region, and the Museum of Ceramics, which is a repository of ancient pottery and clay relics of past civilizations now submerged in time. The Museum of Science and Technology leaves the past for the present and future — and the Lasky Planetarium focuses on the celestial.

As with the Museum of the Diaspora, admission is free on Saturdays from 10am to 2pm. Normal daily hours are from 9am to 4pm, and until 1pm on Fridays. There are also daily shows at the Planetarium at 10, 11 and 12 noon.

There are four separate Tel Aviv museums which concentrate not so much on the ancient past of the country as on the turbulent period leading to independence in 1948, each focusing on a different aspect of the struggle. Taken together, what emerges is a coherent, decisive account of how a small, occupied country managed not only to declare its statehood, but succeeded in successfully resisting the onslaught of enemies many times more numerous.

The Haganah Museum is at 23 Rothschild Boulevard in the center of the city, and deals with the shadowy army that was precursor to the Israel Defense Forces. The acknowledged defense arm of the Palestine Jewish community, Haganah was strictly illegal during the British Mandate period. All of its activities were conducted clandestinely and included acquiring and manufacturing arms, military training, and illicit operations to smuggle Jewish immigrants into the country. There are photos, documents, scale models, uniforms and samples of the weaponry prepared in underground workshops. The hidden caches of hand grenades and Sten guns later used to stem the Arab attacks are exhibited in the building, which was

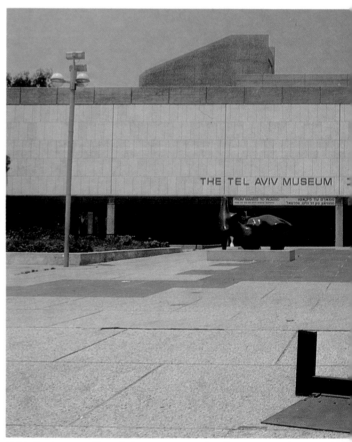

Tel Aviv Museum offers the finest in national and international art.

donated by a former Haganah general. There is material on the 1937 Arab pogroms against the Jews, information about the World War II Jewish brigade which fought the Axis first in North Africa and then in Italy and accounts of Israel's military exploits in all the ensuing wars since its independence.

Closed on Saturday, this museum is open weekdays from 9am to 3pm and until 12.30 on Fridays.

It is impossible to recall Haganah without conjuring up images of Israel's first prime minister; the David Ben-Gurion Museum can be found in his former house on the avenue carrying his name and comprises part of a library and archive reflecting on the extraordinary period prior to and immediately after the birth of Israel. Ben-Gurion bequeathed over 20 000 books to the museum and the house is full of his personal items.

Daily morning hours are from 8am to 1pm and then from 5–7pm on Mondays and Thursdays. There are also Saturday winter hours from 10am to 1pm.

During the stormy period prior to independence, there were two underground armies, often vilified by the rest of the Jewish community of Palestine, that were locked in unrelenting struggle against the British Mandate. The prophet and protagonist of both armies and of armed resistance in general was Vladimir Zeev Jabotinsky; his monument stands at 38 King George Street. Jabotinsky was a fighter and a dreamer. He was absolutely committed to the belief that there would be a Jewish homeland one day and that independence

could be achieved with the sword. He was the spirit behind the Revisionist Zionist Movement, the Betar youth organization, the underground Irgun Zvai Leumi army which fought the Mandate authority for years and which spawned the even more radical and irreconcilable Lehi organization. He was a poet, writer, journalist and soldier whose very name was anathema to Ben-Gurion.

The Jabotinksy Institute deals with his life and the history of all the modern Jewish resistance movements in Palestine including the clandestine Nili, which was formed to assist the British to oust the Turks from the country during World War I. Photos, archives and historical documents are available at the institute, which is open Sunday, Tuesday and Thursday from 8am to 3pm, Mondays and Wednesdays from 8am to 1pm and again from 6–8pm, and on Fridays from 8am to 1pm.

One other musuem which reflects on the period from the vantage point of armed Jewish resistance is strategically sited in what used to be the no-man's land separating the Arabs of Jaffa from the Jewish community in Tel Aviv. Located in a modern glass building facing the sea, the Etzel (or Irgun Zvai Leumi) Museum deals with the confrontations of the underground army first with the British and then with the attacking Arabs. Photos and documents focus on a critical slice of recent history that is both heroic and tragic.

Our museum tour is not over, however; Tel Aviv still has much to show. There is the Museum of the History of Tel Aviv on Bialik Street in the old part of the city, which deals with the founding of the first all-Jewish city in modern history; the Beth Bialik Museum, on the same street, deals with the Hebrew language's foremost poet and writer. If the theater is of interest, the Israel Theater Museum at 3 Melchet Street contains all the historical memorabilia taken from Jewry's distant thespian past and leading up to its present.There are also some very fine photography exhibitions frequently provided by Beth Sokolov Journalists' House on Kaplan Street not far from Hakirya, Israel's Pentagon — and just across the street dividing Tel Aviv from Ramat Gan in the Diamond Exchange, is the Harry Oppenheimer Diamond Museum. Opened in July 1986, his museum explains the history and use of diamonds from time immemorial to the present.

From the Diaspora Museum to Impressionist art exhibitions, from shards of ancient pottery to Phoenician glassware, from Haganah archives to photos of the battle for supremacy of Tel Aviv-Jaffa — this city has so much to offer everyone. □

Born in Vienna, Franz Asherman relocated to Israel when still in his early twenties and has been a devotee of the Tel Aviv museum circuit ever since. His articles frequently appear in European publications.

Safari in the City

THE 225-acre safari park and zoological center in Ramat Gan is only 15 minutes from downtown Tel Aviv. Owned jointly by the two municipalities, it serves the needs of both cities and is a great tourist attraction already catering to approximately half a million visitors every year. Opened in 1983 with many animals which were transferred from the now defunct Tel Aviv Zoo, the open park contains 66 species of mammals and 67 varieties of birds. There are African elephants and Asian pachyderms alongside rhinos, gnus and zebras, all sharing an environment where the animals are mostly free — while their observers are pretty much constrained.

The scenery is lush and green and cool. There are hibiscus and bougainvillea among the many shrubs and trees growing in the safari park. There are ducks and pelicans actually fishing in the pond, and beautiful flamingos flashing pink as they pass. And there are prides of lions in the tall grass not far from wild jungle cats. There are more than one thousand animals in the zoological garden and, most important, they are unfettered and uncaged.

The entrance gate opens at 9am. Tickets are sold until one or two in the afternoon, depending on the season. Visitors may remain in the area until dusk. ☐

The animals run free in the safari park and zoological center run jointly by the municipalities of Tel Aviv and Ramat Gan.

A sporting chance

Israeli writer *Saul Simons* **pokes a little
fun at Tel Avivians in this account of 'the
lack of sports' in their city.**

THE Land of Miracles is also the Land of Paradoxes and so Tel Aviv, the city of sun and surf, is a good reason why the Israeli army is worried. Perhaps it all began when an etymologically-inclined professor at Tel Aviv University announced that athletics was another way of describing exertion, and — besides — that it was a Greek word that had nothing to do with the Chosen People. Whatever the cause, the Israel Defense Forces — the IDF — noted that the overwhelming majority of reservists reporting for annual duty were "a mess".

This was not exactly a new revelation, as it isn't all that unusual for Mediterranean men to trade muscle for fat. But what was alarming, however, was the early rate of decline which meant that atrophy and belly bulges were settling in a lot earlier than expected — too often in the mid-twenties.

Now these conclusions seemed strange for a number of reasons, particularly when referring to Tel Avivians. In the first instance, every male, from toddling to tottering, is reared on the beaches, where healthy exercises are not only encouraged, but are an implicit part of Israeli manhood. Next, no one could possibly convince me that my brethren are not a sports-minded, sports-loving people. When Maccabi-Tel Aviv won the European basketball championship,

The generation gap in Tel Aviv. But just who is fitter than who?

the subsequent euphoria would not have seemed excessive had limitless reserves of oil been discovered beneath the Central Bus Station. Everyone quickly forgot that there were four Americans recruited for the mission.

Soccer is not only the national sport — it is the national obsession. The Eleventh Commandment in most Israeli homes is: "Thou shalt not disturb the viewer between goals except if the house is on fire."

Actually, the more I thought of the army's petulant conclusions, the angrier I got. The whole thing was absurd. How could a nation that produced tennis champion Shlomo Glickstein, Olympic candidates for sailing competitions and even squash players be accused of physical disregard?

I decided, therefore, to investigate the matter thoroughly and then demand an official retraction from the army. Obviously, I would begin with Willi Braunstein, who was the only person I knew who swam in the summer, skied in the winter, volleyballed when it rained and was an ambidextrous tennis player.

"So, Willi," I said, while activating my pocketsized Sony recorder, "do you agree that the latest statements from the IDF indicate a complete disregard of the facts?"

"They are anti-Semites," he replied. "They wish to worry us to death. And they are against Tel Aviv."

I felt a great surge of righteous indignation. "We have tennis courts," I averred.

"And the Yad Eliahu Stadium," added Willi.

"We have surfing," I stated heatedly.

"And wind," he added.

"Tel Aviv has a marina that would have pleased Onassis."

"If he hadn't died," corrected Willi.

"Tell me about the Tel Aviv Ski Club of which you are the president," I said.

"We are nine."

"And you ski?"

"That is not the purpose of the club, since skiing can be a dangerous, antisocial sport. Mostly we yodel. No

one has ever broken a leg yodelling."

"But yodelling doesn't exercise the body," I protested. "You think your voice box is extraterrestrial?" he countered.

I left Willi feeling only partially vindicated. Since the beach was only two streets away, I calculated that it was time for some fieldwork. If ever there was a repository of Israeli machismo, this was it. Fortunately, I quickly spied Moshe the Matkot Mavin, the almost legendary champion of one of Israel's most indigenous and ingenious sports — matkot — which entails ferociously slamming a hard ball with a ping pong paddle at your opponent's nose, usually at the beach.

"We have been sullied by the IDF," I told him.

"Ask your questions," he said immediately. "I will pull no paddles."

"Is matkot an Israeli sport?"

"Is chicken soup Jewish?"

"Is it selective or popular."

"Both!"

"Explain yourself."

"Two people hit the ball. That is selective. Dozens of people avoid being beaned. That is popular."

"In other words, the sport provides general athletics for the masses."

"I couldn't have said it better."

"People are straining and tensing."

"Especially the non-players."

"Is there danger?"

"Only to the spectators."

"Then you disagree with the verdict of the army, Moshe?"

"Emphatically."

I could have continued the line of questioning all day except a tennis ball collided with my Gucci sunglasses, temporarily blinding me. "Miscreant," I called out to the nine-year-old kid who had almost unsighted me.

"Easy", counselled Moshe the Matkot Mavin. "This is a free beach in a free country. Slamming balls on people is the inherent right of every local child. And besides, you were concerned with the quality of sports in the country. Well, here it is. Hit you right on the face."

Passing through the matkot minefields, I spied three young men, presumably all in their late twenties, all showing abdominal bulges that in another sex would have been construed as pregnancy. After explaining my mission, I asked if they swam.

"Of course," they replied in unison.

"Then why aren't you in the water?"

"Medusas," the first replied.

"But that was last year," I protested. Maybe they linger.

"And you?" I asked the second.

"Water irritates my sinuses," he explained.

The third rolled his eyes. "I just ate two hours ago. You want I should get a heart attack?"

"Then I don't understand why the three of you come to the beach," I said.

"We're bird watchers," they laughed.

Tel Aviv is full of health clubs. Almost every major hotel has one. And there is the Tel Aviv Country Club, which produces some of the nation's most intense automotive congestion on Friday afternoons. If I couldn't find the answer at the beach, then certainly I would find it in the sauna.

"Jerry," I asked a health club manager, "how is business?"

"Fantastic," he replied.

"Membership full?"

"Full. Full. Full."

"Then what do you think about what the army said about the poor physical condition of young Israeli males?"

"They're right on the ball."

"But health clubs are prospering," I protested.

"Listen, *boychicle*," explained Jerry. "This is a land of devolution. You learn to play ball when you're a kid. Then you go in to the army and they walk your feet off so you swear never to use your legs except to step into a car. More likely than not, you get an office job and your only exercise is sliding from one chair to another or shoving a sandwich into your mouth. You begin putting on a little weight and you decide to exercise. But the beach is out because they tell you that the ultraviolet rays will kill you. You figure you'll jog and then you learn that your best friend got run over doing just that in north Tel Aviv.

"So you figure that you'll straighten out in the army and you're shocked when you come back three kilos heavier than when you left because you took all your misery and loneliness out on waffles and chocolate bars."

"But . . ."

"Don't interrupt. So you get fatter and flabbier. You breathe hard when you have to climb up stairs and you sweat every time you pick up something heavier than a packet of cigarettes. Your muscles melt into fat and your gut droops. Your only satisfaction is that all your friends are in the same condition, or worse."

"But what about the health club membership?" I could no longer restrain myself.

"That's the whole point. Consciousness of body abuse begins in the fifties, intensifies in the sixties, and reaches an apex in the seventies and eighties. If you make 90, you are practically indestructible."

"Then the health clubs are full of senior citizens?"

"Precisely."

"And the army is right?"

"Exactly."

"And the answer . . .?"

Is to recruit octogenarians, obviously.   □

Saul Simons is an Israeli pedagogue, lecturer and occasional satirist, who could not resist writing a spoof about athletics in his home town.

Members of Israel's 1988 Olympic beachcombing squad limber up before a gruelling practice session.

Art, artists and

One of Israel's top painters, Jean David, has been living and painting in Tel Aviv since 1955. He airs his views in this interview with *Hanoch Ben-Joseph*.

"OF course, an artist is inspired by his environment," he explained patiently, pointing a thin finger toward the large living room window overlooking Hayarkon Street and the Mediterranean. "I have been living and painting in Tel Aviv since 1955 and always I have remained close to the sea. Bodies of water, you see, exert magnetic influences on me. I find everything about the sea interesting — the changing colors, the startlingly original forms of the fish, the shapes of the boats, the waves. The sea inspires me and I love all its facets, whether merely observing or sailing or fishing."

Approaching his eightieth birthday a year before Tel Aviv celebrates its own, Jean David, renowned Israeli painter and designer, stared hard at the surf colliding with the bodies of swimmers three storeys below, just across the street. "Without the sea, my whole life would have been different. I would either be dead or painting smiling workmen producing Rumanian tractors. I knew the fates of too many artists in Rumania. They either succumbed, starved or went to prison.

"It was the Black Sea that provided the only exit out of hell for me and for 12 other Jews who were trapped by the Nazis in 1942. We purchased a boat from a sympathetic Greek in Constanza in February, arriving in Beirut six months later. Then the British towed us to Cyprus and finally I arrived in Palestine, joining first the Royal Navy, and then the Israel Navy after the state was declared. It was also the sea that brought me to the Greek islands year after year, season after season. The islands were inspiring for me. After each visit, I could return recharged, a little richer for the experience."

Tel Aviv is a city rich in art, artists, galleries and museums and I wanted Jean David to comment on them. Surely, there were one hundred galleries within easy walking distance of his apartment, and in Jaffa and the famous Dizengoff cafes where artists met and exchanged ideas were just behind us. Art was not only a flourishing subject in the city, but also big business. People often traveled thousands of kilometers in order to purchase specific paintings or sculpture. This phenomenon eased life for artists like Bucharest-born David, whose first public display in the country was in 1946, and whose works have since been shown in

Red morning. Oil on canvas, 130 × 120cm. Singapore Hotel.

72

artistry

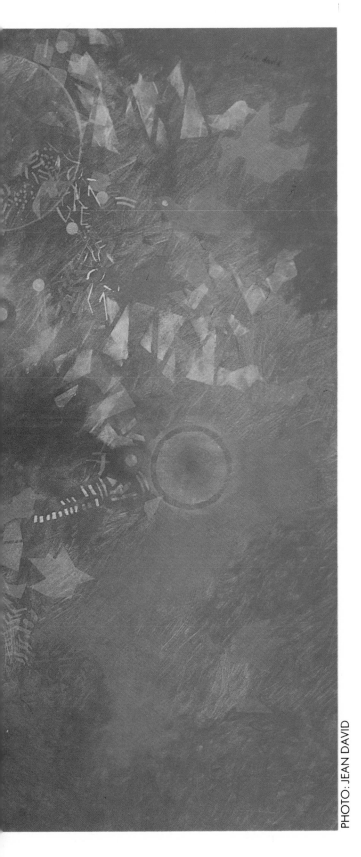

nearly all the principal cities of the western world — fetching prices anywhere from $2000 to $30 000, depending on size and the amount of work involved.

"In many respects," smiled the artist, "I am a very atypical painter. What really interests me is not the work of others, but my own forms of expression. True, you can learn quite a lot from exposure to other artists. This was fine when I was studying at the Ecole des Beaux Arts in Paris as a young man and thirsting for new ideas and techniques. Now I really don't feel the need to discuss art or to be influenced or changed by the works of others — or even to maintain contacts with galleries. I am really concerned with what is locked up in my head."

"Yet you have to sell," I suggested.

"I don't have to do anything," he corrected, "except express myself honestly and as correctly as I can. Anyway, I haven't had trouble selling my paintings for years — usually because potential buyers know my work or me prior to any discussions."

Was there such a thing as "Jewish" or "Israeli" art, I wanted to know. After all, Jean David has honed his skills with such now legendary artists as Marcel Janco, Reuven Rubin, Mordechai Ardon, Nahum Gutman and Moshe Castel.

"No," he replied. "There are Jewish themes, much the same as there have been Christian themes or pastoral subjects or landscapes. It's obvious that if Israeli artists are living in Jerusalem or Tel Aviv or Safed, they will be influenced by what they see around them. But to confuse this with schools of art or 'movements' is simply stupid. I, for one, still get my inspiration from Europe and the Greek islands."

I knew that one of the most striking features of the man with the white hair and youthful eyes seated opposite me was his success not only as a painter, but as a designer. Jean David's murals decorated El Al's first aircraft and the tradition continued right up until, and including, the Boeing 747. He designed reliefs and provided paintings for Zim passenger ships when they were still in the business of carrying people instead of cargo. The first impression visitors glean from the Technion's Churchill Auditorium is a Jean David mural; his works similarly decorate the Weizmann Institute in Rehovot and the Hebrew University in Jerusalem.

"There were periods in my life," he affirmed, "when I was more concerned with graphics and design than with painting. I made lots of money. I enjoyed myself. I also knew that sooner or later I would return to fine art. And that's what happened although lots of years passed in the interim."

What about the artistic excitement of Tel Aviv, I wanted to know. The city was virtually awash with young, new talent. Studios were breeding a generation

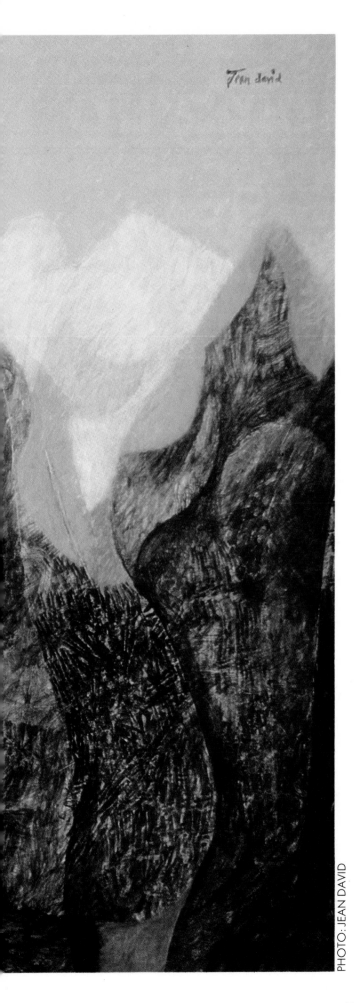

*The flower-eater. Oil on canvas, 130 × 97cm.
Private collection, New York.*

of inquisitive minds who were translating novel ideas into colors and forms on canvas. Hardly a day passed in Tel Aviv without at least one new exhibition announced in the plethora of galleries around Gordon Street. What did it all mean?

"What it means," said Jean David, "is that we have quantity. We have vast numbers of young people who consider themselves artists and, because of the large number of galleries in the city, have a fair chance of exhibiting and even selling. It also means that we have plenty of cafes where people can talk a lot. What it doesn't mean is that we are really producing art, that fine new painters are emerging, that after the distillation of quantity, there will be quality. Only time will tell."

It was interesting that so many of Israel's really great artists were of Rumanian origin and that, like Janco, Rubin and David, much of their artistic life had been spent in Tel Aviv. Rubin, for example, took particular joy in painting the city as it grew from a sandy village into a mighty metropolis. once he wrote: "Art is an expression of love. I paint what I love, my country, my people . . ."

"There is nothing very extraordinary about the phenomenon," explained the painter. "Paris was the art center of the world when we grew up and Rumanians were deeply influenced by French culture. Also a high proportion of Rumanian Jews survived. Other communities were not so fortunate. Since artists are usually fairly individualistic, they respond differently to situations. Rubin, who was Israel's first ambassador to Rumania, was far more extroverted than some of the others. I, on the other hand, find less need to talk and more compulsion to work as I grow older. I simply have no patience for distractions. There is still so much to be expressed and there is not enough time — there never is."

I still wanted to find out how Jean David felt about Tel Aviv. There were other Israeli cities close to the sea he appreciated so deeply. "Well, I guess the fact that I have been coming back for 33 years must mean something," he said, smiling.

The meeting was over. The lure of the sea and the easel was too strong for this puny interviewer.   ☐

Hanoch Ben-Joseph, a freelance journalist, was born in Israel before there was an Israel. Jean David is one of his favorite artists.

Shaping up Israel

The renowned Israeli sculptress, Ziva Caspi, represents yet another facet of Tel Aviv — exciting and provocative art. Photographer *Yigal Zaken* not only took the photographs, but also wrote this piece.

TEL AVIV has been a focal point of Israeli art and artists for decades. The galleries, the museums, and the inherent excitement of the country's most scintillating city all contribute to the spirit of creative endeavors.

Ziva Caspi is a sculptress of rare talent who has both studied her craft, and exhibited her work in Tel Aviv, and whose much-praised works are shown twice yearly at the Tel Aviv Dan Hotel. The city has played a crucial role in her life; born in Siberia in 1944, and a member of Kibbutz Afek by the time she was 13, the artist attended the Avni School of Art in Tel Aviv as a young adult, and this proved to be a turning point in her life. Two of the most important women in Israeli sculpture — Batia Lishansky and Hana Orloff — discovered her there, encouraging her to persevere with her craft.

Praised by critics both in Israel and throughout Europe for her "assured technique, sensitivity, delicacy, and outstanding skill," the artist explained: "My sculptural world is one of bodies, multiple faces and opposite emotions. Like the living body, the sculptural one is the substance of emotion — by which I mean that it gives emotion a body's pliancy and three-dimensionality, and the body, an emotion's distinctiveness and pain or pleasure."

In addition to her many successful foreign and local exhibitions, the artist was chosen by the government's Coins and Medallion Corporation to design a special coin praising motherhood — an assignment which this mother of three particularly welcomed.

An extraordinary spirit, Ziva Caspi may no longer be a resident of Tel Aviv, but she most certainly is a product of the city, joined by thousands of other bright and creative artists who together make the metropolis one of the world's leading art centers. □

77

Shopping in Tel Aviv-Jaffa is not only worthwhile — it can be lots of fun, according to *Helen Kaye*, **who has been covering the subject for years.**

The quest for bargains

One of the most modern shopping centers in the country is appropriately located in Dizengoff Center which is both central and chic.

WELCOME to a guided shopping tour of Tel Aviv, Israel's bustling city by the sea. Although these are not the only places we shall visit, Dizengoff, Ben Yehuda and Allenby are the city's major shopping streets. The former is the most fashionable of the three, especially for clothing and footwear — which follow European fashion trends. At its southern end the Dizengoff Center is a huge three-storey shopping mall straddling both sides of the street.

Ben Yehuda runs parallel to Dizengoff one block over from Hayarkon, where Tel Aviv's luxury hotels are situated. Most of Tel Aviv's furriers have their stores here, many of them clustered near the southern end where Ben Yehuda decants into Allenby.

Running right down to the beaches and curving round to lie in the same south-north line as its sister streets, Allenby shares with Ben Yehuda most of Tel Aviv's jewelry, arts and crafts and gift stores, although Dizengoff too has a goodly number. Halfway up Allenby is the rambunctious Carmel Market, where you

can buy fresh-this-morning produce and fruit, seasonal flowers and bulbs for a pittance. So with all this in mind, take a map, a hat and a smile and sally forth.

The first stop on Allenby is one of the city's finest café-bakeries at No.47 — Kapulski Bros — where calorie-rich confections have been made for more than 50 years. Here you can have a cup of coffee — or a glass of tea with lemon in the old way — before continuing your search for the lovely products Israel makes for you to buy in Tel Aviv.

The old way! It seems that you can turn up the past anywhere in Israel with each spade of soil. Antiquities are fun to own and to give. A small oil lamp of red clay lies in your palm like a quiet mystery. Whose hands trimmed its wick, or filled it with oil?

Reputable antiquities dealers are licensed by the government. Each artifact is entered in a register monitored by the appropriate ministry and the buyer is given a certificate of authenticity. Guv's Gallery at 88 HaYarkon Street has lamps, juglets and other items dating from the Early Bronze Age (3000BCE) to the ninth century CE. "Guv" is Irwin Driman, a former stockbroker whose shop supplants his once sober office. He is thought of as something of an authority on ancient coins, which he sells as is or mounted in gold and silver. Prices start at about $50. The delicate Roman glass at Guv's dates from the first and third centuries CE. Prices start around $30 and vary according to the age or rarity of the object.

Didya Antiques at 5 Mazal Dagim in Old Jaffa has a selection of lamps and juglets dating from the Middle Bronze to the Byzantine eras. There are also bronze figurines from the second century BCE to the first century CE, Roman glass vials, and even spear and arrowheads for the weapons buff.

Roman glass vessels are, of course, more costly than the clay lamps and juglets and usually start at around $100; their intriguing iridescence is caused by oxidation. Didya also has a lovely selection of contemporary jewelry that has been crafted around shards of Roman

Citroën BX.

DAVID LUBINSKI LTD - CONCESSIONNAIRE EXCLUSIF

glass. These items are priced at around $100.

The shopping district of Old Jaffa, itself well worth a visit, is a honeycomb of alleys — all named for the signs of the Zodiac — which contain the stores, galleries and studios of Tel Aviv artists and craftspeople whose work is available for sale. These include Handelman silk-screen prints at 14 Mazal Dagim ($25 and up) and the gallery of famed sculptor Frank Meisler at 25 Simtat Arie. Meisler's plaques, figures, boxes and other creations have a delicious sense of humor and, very often, moving parts. The price of these works of art can run into hundreds of dollars but can only appreciate in value.

The Wizo stores are at 87 Allenby and 94 Ben Yehuda. Maskit have a shop in the El Al building on Ben Yehuda Street and a handsome new store on the corner of Frischmann Street. Wizo and Maskit shops are dedicated to showcasing Israeli artists, both traditional and contemporary. Wizo specializes in ethnic crafts and has a beautiful selection of Yemenite jewelry in silver and gilt. Prices start at $20. Maskit also has a large jewelry department, as well as exclusive local pottery, weaves, and designer clothing. Maskit is generally more upmarket in prices, but there are also items to suit a modest purse.

The Miller stores at 157 and 169 Dizengoff have a splendid collection of Roman glass and other jewelry, consisting of one-off pieces made by the artists Miller commissions. These pieces start at around $150.

Jewelry is altogether a good buy in Israel, selling for 20 to 30 per cent less than equivalent items in Europe or the USA. Pearls, coral, hemetite, onyx and the rich

Sophisticated, comprehensive shopping centers are relatively new phenomena in Tel Aviv, but have become exceedingly popular over the past decade. The Canyon Shopping Center, just across the border in Ramat Gan, is an indication of what modern Tel Aviv shopping is all about — boutiques, supermarkets, restaurants, cafes all conveniently housed under a single roof thanks to the foresight of Canadian-Israeli architect and investor David Azrieli.

indigo lapis are available and very popular. Dizengoff is the preferred hunting ground, but Allenby too has a number of reputable (*surely* there is no other kind?) jewelry stores. Fuhrer at No. 73 specialize in traditional pieces — they mix and match corals and pearls, jade and onyx, gold and lapis. Because lapis is easy to fake, buyers should make sure the item they purchase is not dyed or flawed.

When buying jewelry, forget the little shop on the corner whose owner promises incredible bargains. Jewelry prices vary with the quality and size of the stone. Quantity and design add to the total.

Many years ago a wise finance minister realized that for the fur trade to flourish in Israel — just the thought of fur on the average August day in Tel Aviv would make anyone wilt — he would have to do something. He did — and you, the visitor to Israel, can benefit as a result, because there are no customs duties on furs.

Anna Grenfor (80 Ben Yehuda) and Ronar (74 Ben Yehuda) typify the couturier furrier of Tel Aviv. Grenfor furs are flamboyant, sensual, generously proportioned and imaginative. Ronar's coats have a fluid elegance of line and indefinable flair. Both furriers show their

GOTTEX MODELS LTD. 62 MORDEKHAI ANNU EVITCH STREET P.O.B. 9233 TEL AVIV 67060 ISRAEL

collections in October of every year.

Montatel, at No.76, purchases designs from London fashion houses which are applied in his workshops above the store, while the dean of Israeli furriers and an international legend in his own right is Stefan Braun at 99 Allenby. This street was once Tel Aviv's premier shopping street — and 99 is still a noteworthy address for lovers of exquisite furs.

Furriers are tiresomely reluctant when it comes to drawing out prices, however. They won't tell. A Greenland blue fox jacket could cost $1000, a full length mink $3500, a Russian lynx $10 000 — but there are too many variables that go into the making of a fur for it to be priced like a box of cornflakes. Mutual trust must prevail.

Israel has long been famous for its leather apparel for men and women. Beged-Or represents the ultimate in classic design while Gingette offers high-fashion model garments in a material that was once thought to be fit only for flying jackets and Buffalo Bill.

Both companies — the Gingette store is called Jet — are represented in stores at the Dizengoff Center and are virtually next to one another. Up the road, at 99 King George Street, is Tadmor. King George runs at right angles to the Dizengoff Center, also flowing into Allenby and the Carmel Market. Prices average around $300 for skirts, are slightly lower for pants, and higher for jackets. These prices are reduced by 25 per cent when payment is made in foreign currency.

If you visit Tel Aviv in the summer, bathing suits are a good buy. Israel's foremost swimwear designers, Diva, Gottex and Gideon Oberson, all have their

factories and showrooms in the Tel Aviv area. The average price of one of their suits is in the range of $55 to $95. HaMashbir in the Dizengoff Center stocks all the name brands as does Kol-Bo Shalom, the big department store in the Shalom tower just off Allenby. Another famous bathing suit address in Tel Aviv is Salon Malca, at 160 Dizengoff, where a small army of seamstresses will alter your swimsuit on the spot if need be. It's also worth noting that Gottex makes good-looking suits especially for the fuller figure or the older woman.

Have you ever thought of buying skincare products from Israel? Dead Sea Drugs (DSD) and Ahava manufacture a full line of skincare products for every type of skin. These government-approved and tested products contain vivifying chemicals from the Dead Sea, which is the world's lowest point below sea level. DSD even has a special cream for feet; 112 grams cost about $3.60. You can buy all these products at HaMashbir and the better drugstores in the city.

Perfumes or gifts? Nobody can quite decide how to classify Judith Muller's fragrances. Muller herself resolves the dilemma by offering gift packages of Batsheva, Shalom and Judith in duos, trios or each by itself with a painted glass ornament. All the fragrances are florals and come in specially painted glass flagons, as does the mens' line, which is called King David and sells for $8 and up. All these perfumes can be found at Maskit and also at cosmetics counters. A break? Of course. Time to stop at one of Dizengoff's many cafés for fresh orange juice or perhaps a can of Galil pure apple cider while we consider wines.

People are beginning to recognize the light perfections of the Golan Heights Wineries, whose Yarden, Golan and Gamla vintages are sold in supermarkets and liquor stores all over town. Another newcomer is Hallelujah, a delicious orange brandy made by Askelon that tastes much like Grand Marnier. And, of course, there is Sabra, Israel's famed chocolate orange liqueur. The wines cost around $9 and the liqueurs, around $8.

If you are looking for Judaica you will find candlesticks, *mezuza* casings, *kiddush* cups and other devotional objects at Maskit, Wizo and in the many stores on Ben Yehuda and Allenby, and of course in Old Jaffa. Check to see whether these are locally made before you buy. The silver objects are often silver plated and are therefore inexpensive, while a sculpted sterling silver candlestick starts at around $250.

It makes sense, however, to go to a nearby suburb of Tel Aviv proper, called Bnei Brak, for Judaica. Its main street, Rabbi Akiva, has many such shops. Bnei Brak is an observant community, so dress modestly. At Rabbi Akiva 95 (the store doesn't seem to have a name) is a great collection of silver and silver-plated devotional objects from around $18.

Last, before we say *lehitraot* — Hebrew for see you again — there are two stores that epitomize the many shops run by young Israeli designers and artists.

At April (97 King George Street), Daniella Kadish and Michal Shamir make casually elegant women's clothing out of cotton, cotton knits, linens and other easy-care fabrics. These are individually hand-painted in a variety of designs — from whimsical animals to abstract shapes. Shamir has a deft and delicate flair for color and will paint designs to order. New collections emerge in spring and fall and the clothes are reasonably priced.

Plastic Plus is at 30 Shenkin Street, an artery running east from Allenby just opposite the Carmel Market. Shenkin is one of Tel Aviv's oldest streets and its houses and stores are gradually being sequestered by bright and energetic young people. At Plastic Plus, Hans Pallada and his wife Elana Herschenberg make cheeky yet graceful high-tech-influenced articles for home and office. From memo holders to floor lamps in bright primary colors, the products are sturdy and well made — and the prices are reasonable.

Finally, it should be noted that many Tel Aviv shops close between 1–4pm, although Dizengoff stores are open all day. The prices quoted are approximate and subject to change. Anyone paying in foreign currency will not be subject to value added tax (VAT) or purchase tax. Your purchases would normally be delivered to you at Ben-Gurion Airport prior to departure. Tel Aviv offers a gallimaufry of shopping pleasures. Have fun. □

Helen Kaye had a diverse background before she began writing about shopping regularly for the Jerusalem Post. She is regarded as one of Israel's leading authorities on consumer topics.

Carmel Market, Allenby Street.
Kapulski Bros, 47 Allenby Street.
Guv's Gallery, 88 HaYarkon Street.
Didya Antiques, 5 Mazal Dagim, Old Jaffa.
14 Mazal Dagim, Old Jaffa.
Meisler Gallery, 25 Simtat Arie.
Wizo, 87 Allenby Street, and 94 Ben Yehuda Street.
Maskit, Frischmann Street, and El Al Building,
    Ben Yehuda Street.
Miller Galleries, 157 and 169 Dizengoff Street.
Fuhrer, 73 Allenby street.
Anna Grenfor, 80 Ben Yehuda.
Rona, 74 Ben Yehuda.
Montatel, 76 Ben Yehuda.
Stefan Braun, 99 Allenby Street.
Beg ed-Or, Dizengoff Center.
Jet, Dizengoff Center.
Tadmor, 99 King George Street.
HaMashbir, Dizengoff Center.
Kol-Bo Shalom, Shalom Tower, off Allenby Street.
Salon Malca, 160 Dizengoff Street.
95 Rabbi Akiva, Bnei Brak.
April, 97 King George Street.
Plastic Plus, 30 Shenkin Street.

Picturesque anarchy in the Central Bus Station.

Gali®

The Champion of sport fashion in Israel

Available at "Gali" Stores:

"Gali" – 173 Dizengoff st. Tel Aviv
"Gali" – Dizengoff Center, Tel Aviv
"Gali" – Canyon Ayalon – Ramat-Gan

Design by: Shuky Levy.

The Tel Aviv area is one of the world's most important diamond centers. *Paul Hirschhorn* **looks into the glittering world of gems.**

THE huge sign on the side of the three towering high rises which house the Israel Diamond Exchange in Ramat Gan near Tel Aviv proclaims Israel as the "world's number one exporter" of polished diamonds.

Diamonds are indeed a major Israeli enterprise. Approximately 9000 polishers are employed by the industry in hundreds of factories. Dozens of new diamond-processing plants are opened in Israel each year and it all adds up to big business. Diamond exports have been growing in recent years, totalling around $1.2 billion annually. Approximately 60 per cent of production is now destined for sale on the American market, according to Moshe Schnitzer, president of the Israeli Diamond Exchange.

While America is an established, "traditional" market, Israel's prowess in the field is in continually opening new market horizons: total annual exports of all goods to Japan, for example, is about $185 million. Despite the attention paid to Israel's high technology, however, a full 69 per cent of these exports is diamonds. Japan is the country's third largest diamond customer, after Hong Kong, which buys about 11 per cent of Israeli exports. Other major nations doing significant business with Israeli diamantaires include Belgium, Switzerland, Canada, the United Kingdom, West Germany, France, Italy, Singapore and Holland. Success in these markets has made Israel one of the major purchasers of the rough diamonds sold by the Central Selling Organization (CSO), based in London, and known commonly in the industry as the "Syndicate". According to Zvi Shur, director general of the Diamond Manufacturers Association, "Israeli diamantaires buy more than 50 per cent of the rough diamonds sold by the Diamond Syndicate. Of the $1.6 billion sold by the Syndicate, $900 million is purchased by Israel, although not all of it directly."

Israel's major position in the world industry, along with the long ties held between Jews and diamonds, led to the opening of the Harry Oppenheimer Museum during the 23rd World Diamond Congress held in Israel in 1986. Located near the Israeli diamond bourse, the museum's exhibits on the diamond industry and on the Jewish role in this activity have made it one of Tel Aviv's newest tourist attractions, visited not only by foreign buyers visiting Israel to make purchases or sales, but also by non-diamantaires.

"The museum is an attractive forum for providing a window on what is certainly one of the most secretive of the world's major industries," says Gordon Shifman, an Israeli journalist who specializes in the diamond industry and has written for two of the country's major diamond publications. "The exhibits include a di-

Diamonds in the rough

Various cuts of diamonds: Emerald, Pear, Brilliant, Marquise and Baguette.

PHOTO COURTESY OF DE BEERS

amond mine model and exhibits of diamond-cutting and polishing equipment throughout the centuries, exhibits of actual and facsimile gems, descriptions with pictorial accompaniments of the diamond-trading process, and a good film on the history of diamonds. They always have a traveling exhibit which includes a replica of the Crown Jewels, the breastplate of the high priest, world-winning entries in diamond jewelry contests, and more. And the museum also has a library on diamond subjects."

Taken in historic context the decision to open a diamond museum in Tel Aviv should come as no surprise. The Jewish connection with diamonds appeared in medieval times and has been traced back to the Biblical world. There are references in the Bible to the "diamond" (Hebrew, *yahalom*) in the breastplate of the high priest in Exodus (28:18), the stones of fire of Ezekiel, and Jeremiah's diamond penpoint. The translation of the word "diamond" in this period is in dispute, and it may have referred to different, exceptionally hard minerals. But some sources believe there is evidence of prehistoric diamond mining, and it has even been suggested that Kimberly might have been the place of origin of the diamonds in the breastplate of the high priest, and of those which the Queen of Sheba offered to King Solomon.

While these points may be debated, it is certain that the strong Jewish ties with the modern diamond trade can be traced back to fourteenth century Venice. During this period, Venice was a vital bridge between the civilizations of the east and west and France was the major market for finished diamonds. Therefore it was logical that diamond-cutting activity should soon begin in Paris. The expansion of the fledgling industry continued in Europe, spreading to Amsterdam, Lisbon, Bruges in Flanders, and Nuremberg. These cities all became important links in the chain of the diamond trade.

The persecutions of the Jews greatly influenced the movement and expansion of the diamond business. The Jews carried their skills with them — one of the main advantages for a persecuted people opting for this particular trade. Another important feature was the trade's international nature, making it a natural choice for people who brought with them experience in international trade, and ties which stretched from Europe to points east. Perhaps most significantly the diamond trade was not closed to Jews, since it was not covered by racial and religious restrictions of the medieval craft guilds. Jews, therefore, entered the diamond trade in great numbers and some observers claim they have dominated it ever since.

Honeywell, Bull and Nec: an extraordinary grafting in the EDP world.

Grafting is a process that permits the combining of the best part of similar plants in order to create one plant capable of bearing exceptional fruits.

. An extraordinary graft occurred on March 27th, 1987, when three companies that for over 20 years have been in the fore-front of the EDP world became one reality: Honeywell, Bull and Nec.

Thanks to their compatibility Honeywell Bull was born. This new name in the EDP world combines all the qualities of three large international companies.

From today this name will be the strength of your business.

Honeywell Bull

MN Medan Computers Ltd.
Sole distributor in Israele - HONEYWELL BULL ITALIA
3 Efal St., Kiryat Arieh - P.O.B. 3005 - Peatch Tikva 49130 ISRAELE

To this day, the phrase *mazel und bracha*, a Yiddish expression meaning "good luck and blessings", is employed along with a handshake to close a deal in diamonds — even between non-Jews. And today, as part of a continuing tradition, Tel Aviv is a major diamond center, along with Amsterdam, Antwerp, London and New York. The ties of the Israeli industry to Jewish history are not only traditional, but organic as well. Jews escaping Nazi persecution in Europe brought their experience to Israel. Netanya, north of Tel Aviv, was a major center for the new industry, and in 1940 that city's mayor, Oved Ben Ami, went to London to help arrange regular supplies of "rough" for the flegling industry. He succeeded, and this led to further expansion. By 1942, there were 2000 people employed in diamond-related endeavors.

Despite the return to Europe of some of the refugees after the war, the Israeli industry continued to grow, and exports rose from a level of $548 million in 1975 to $1.4 billion in 1980. Then the crisis that ravaged the world-wide industry also hit Israel. Notes Zvi Shur: "December, 1982 was the lowest point. Exports dropped to $900 million in the branch. But from then on things have improved. From 1982 on the Israeli industry has been growing. At its peak, there were 15 000 polishers; at its nadir, 6500. Today there are more than 9000 and the number is rising. We are approaching the peak export years again.

"During this period, people changed their attitudes. Until the crisis, the measure of success was the accumulated polished stock of a good diamantaire. After the crisis there was a realization that the stress should be on the best price in the shortest time. There is a need to sell quickly because financing is expensive. Sometimes it is more sensible to sell at a low price than to hold the stock."

The turnaround was aided by a major reorganization. Shur says: "We went from very big organizations, of, for example, 1800 workers, to smaller units. Today the largest is 350 workers. There are some factories of 200, but there are only eight plants with over 100 workers. Altogether there are 700 plants. An estimated 45 per cent of the workers are in factories of 30 or more, 55 per cent of 30 or below."

The climb back to profitability has not been without its difficulties. Among the problems Israel's diamond business has faced are questions of competition with low wage countries, like India. And, in direct contrast to other sectors of Israel's economy, which face growing unemployment, the diamond industry has faced a shortage of trained manpower — a possible bottleneck to future growth. As in other Israeli industries, leaders of Israel's diamond industry are convinced that only with highly trained and motivated manpower can it counter what it lacks in local raw material supplies.

To meet these needs, special vocational programs have been created at several schools in Tel Aviv and the surrounding region. Institutes now offering courses in the subject are the ORT High School in Ramat Gan, the Youth Educational and Vocational Training Center in Netanya, the WIZO Vocational High School in Rehovot, and the Amal School in Petah Tikvah. On the managerial level, there is a training course for managers in Tel Aviv at the Technion External Studies Division. Several dozen diamantaires take part in lectures on technological advances, economics, management, law, and other subjects. Experts in these fields and senior industry figures discuss the history and current status of the industry, government-industry relations, taxes, and other related subjects.

Dealing inside the Israeli Bourse.

In the belief that robots and computers can solve the diamond industry's growing manpower needs, scientific researchers have set their sights on creating a fully automatic diamond plant requiring only one worker to bring in the rough and turn on the electricity to start production. In an industry which is passed from father to son, however, the implementation of new technologies is a slow and careful procedure. A main force behind the introduction of technology is the Israel Diamond Institute, also located in the Tel Aviv area. The Institute is funded by government and industry and in turn provides financing for research. "We introduced the idea that something can be done to improve the technology of working diamonds," explains pioneer of diamond-technology research Professor Yishaya Yarnitsky, of the Technion-Israel Institute of Technology.

Technological developments in the Israeli diamond industry began more than 20 years ago, when a semi-automatic polishing machine was developed. Israeli researchers have also designed a fully automatic machine for polishing 16 facets. Called David 3 and manufactured by Amcoran, a subsidiary of Tel Aviv's Amcor Corporation, the machine divides diamonds with greater accuracy than can be achieved by hand —

On this machine a diamond dust impregnated wheel polishes the facets of several stones.

with one operator serving as many as eight machines at once. Another Israeli invention is called Dafna, a machine produced by both Kulso and Vertikowsky to polish the girdle, the center of the diamond. More than 5000 of these machines are in use around the world today.

Two models of a bruting machine have also been developed. In bruting, a piece of whole diamond, instead of diamond powder, is used to shape another diamond. At present bruting requires employment of the full weight of the bruter's body against a hand-operated machine — whereas the new machine will enable one bruter to operate six to eight machines at the same time. In addition a new sawing machine is in the final developmental stages. It can cut knots (seams between two different crystals in the diamond) that can be hard to work and which often cause the diamond to break.

Technology may solve problems resulting from the wide fluctuation in the number of employees in the industry over the years, but technological advances have not yet revolutionized this most traditional of businesses. Zvi Shur believes nevertheless that new technology will play an important role in the future of the Israeli diamond industry. "One of the subjects of discussion in the business is the process of diamond cutting. In some cases, like the polishing wheel, we are working with the methods of a hundred years ago. It is done in small places, passed on from father to son. This gap is a serious problem. All over the world efforts are being made to change the machines, but I don't know of any breakthrough.

"The two main problems are the relation of the diamond to the wheel and the components. Glue and diamond dust are the polishing materials. You cannot change the diamond, so you must try to have the optimum synthesis of wheel, glue and dust, rpm, velocity. Another area of technological challenge is to try to install a robot to take the place of the cutting worker. This is not simple because rough is so expensive. Until now, only human work has had maximum utility. It's a delicate game. Each change in weight is really the important factor in the polishing business. A range of 2 per cent can mark the difference between profit and loss.

"In this industry, we spend large sums of money for a few percentage points of profit, and the percentage is related to the weight of the stone. If we can use 48 per cent instead of 46 per cent, it can make the difference between profit and loss — 50 per cent is considered good use of rough. Perhaps we will move to laser screening, or an intelligent computer to solve the problem. We have a very high level of technological know-how in Israel, and we must pursue progress in this realm."

In recent years, the recovery of the diamond industry has continued to gather steam, though as one Tel Aviv publication wrote: "diamonds are forever, but the industry has its ups and downs." Shur believes Israeli diamantaires deserve a large share of the credit for the recovery. He says that their response to the crisis was rapid and helped lead the Israeli exchange to its current position of strength. "They adjusted more quickly than all the other diamond-cutting centers in the world and today we are the most important cutting center in the west," he says. Optimism has pervaded in recent years, with one expert crowing that "the industry is seen moving toward a return to the prosperity of the late 1970s."

Moshe Schnitzer, president of the Israel Diamond Exchange, attributed the industry's current strength to the availability of large quantities of the complete range of competitively priced commercial stones in demand on world jewelry markets. Schnitzer said that Israel is by far the most active cutting center in the diamond world today. It also benefits from lowered production costs due to government economic policy which has reduced real wages. Clearly, the industry centered in the three towers overlooking Tel Aviv will continue to make itself felt on international markets. □

Paul Hirschhorn is a freelance journalist who works for the Associated Press and for an American radio network in northern Israel.

WE HANDLE YOUR CARGO LIGHTLY BUT SERIOUSLY.

ZIM —
SERVING ISRAEL'S
COMMERCE
IN 250 PORTS
38 COUNTRIES
6 CONTINENTS

ZIM ISRAEL NAVIGATION Co.

THE TEL AVIV STOCK EXCHANGE LTD.

The Tel Aviv Stock Exchange (TASE) has been since its establishment in 1953, the nerve centre of the Israeli Capital Market and a major instrument for raising capital in Israel. It is regulated and supervised by the Ministry of Finance on one hand, and the Securities Authority on the other.

Four major financial instruments are traded on the Exchange: Shares, Warrants, bonds (public and corporate, the latter including straights as well as convertibles), and short term government paper. The Exchange is considering the introduction of additional financial instruments, particularly futures.

For the past two years, the floor of the Tel Aviv Stock Exchange have known a renewed activity while the institutions of the "bursa" have drastically improved the trading systems and introduced new rules and regulations.

The activity on the Stock Market has attracted foreign investors who have taken advantage of the fact that Israeli exchange control regulations enable them to repatriate both capital and profits from investments in shares.

After the Stock Market collapsed in 1983, it went through a period of hibernation which lasted about two years. By the end of 1985, it went bullish again, with share prices and trading turnover increasing. Between October 1985 and December 1987, share prices went up by approximately 100 per cent in dollar terms, reflecting greater optimism concerning the Israeli economy in general and the Stock Market in particular. New companies are applying for listing with the Exchange in increasing numbers; there are now 283 companies listed on the Tel Aviv Stock Exchange as against 259 at the end of 1983, in spite of the delisting of 26 companies during the same period.

The days of high inflation which were the rule during the first half of the 1980s were replaced by an era of relative stability. The inflation rate declined from approximately 500 per cent a year in 1984 to 16 per cent in 1987. As a result, the profitability of companies improved, investors interest was renewed and savings flowed back to the stock market.

But not to the same stock market. new trading methods were developed: until recently, the only trading system was multilateral where "all the members trade with everybody". Each member of the Exchange matches its customers' buy and sell orders for a given security, and brings the net balance to the Exchange. The members' overall net buy and sell positions are then further pooled together, creating an exchange-wide net supply or demand position which is then the object of trading on the floor.

Last April, The Exchange introduced a new system of trading: the "Variables" trading system, a bilateral form of trading similar to what exists in other

exchanges around the world. It applies to the 25 largest companies. The securities of the other companies are still traded according to the multilateral system. This has increased the efficiency of trading and facilitated the spreading of information among traders and investors alike.

The Exchange set up a parallel market by defining new listing regulations which enabled smaller companies, with a less established track record to be listed on the Exchange. The securities of 56 of such companies are now traded in that framework.

The government, for its part, contributed to the improvement of the climate on capital markets. It started implementing a comprehensive tax reform and relaxed the regulations applying to the issuing of corporate bonds. A relatively large number of issues followed and it is expected that this sector which had been dormant until now will develop.

These changes should ensure that the Tel Aviv Stock Exchange will play a fundamental role in the future growth of the Israeli economy.

$ YIELD INDEX
100 = 31-12-86

167·79
133·14
165·65
83·631
65·569
52·039

O N D J F M A M J J A S O N D J F M A M J J A S O N D
86   87
26-9-85 to 29-10-87

THE TEL AVIV STOCK EXCHANGE LTD.
54 AHAD HAMM STREET, TEL AVIV
ISRAEL 65543
TEL. 03-627 411
TELEX. 34212 TASE

You can bank on it!

Tel Aviv is home base for Israel's Stock Exchange and the head offices of all the nation's banks. *Joseph Morgenstern* **examines two sides of the financial spectrum.**

ISRAELI banking has been characterized for many years by a high level of sophistication, providing comprehensive financial services to companies, institutions and individuals. The banks have been key factors in the growth of the economy, financing its infrastructure, industrial development and international trade, while offering individuals and households various savings and investment channels.

A recent survey of the extent and size of Israeli banking institutions, all headquartered in Tel Aviv, indicated that their total assets and liabilities stood at $56.4 billion. The deposits of the public in local currencies amounted at $28.7 billion, while deposits in foreign currency stood at $13.4 billion. The credit extended by the banking institutions to the general public were $16.5 billion, while credit to the government was $17.6 billion.

Three major banking groups account for 90 per cent of the total assets of banks in Israel. The three groups are Bank Hapoalim, Bank Leumi and Israel Discount Bank; two other significant banks are United Mizrahi Bank and First International. Total assets of the Israeli banks, as of 1986, were $72 billion; their net profit was $17.5 million. During that same period Bank Hapoalim was Israel's largest and most profitable bank, with assets of $26.2 billion — and with a net profit of $16.7 million.

Israel's banks have seen lower levels of profitability in recent years. Lowered interest rates and financial spreads, an imposed near-freeze on banking fees, inordinately high tax rates and continued difficulties on the part of various business sectors have necessitated large provisions for doubtful debts. The banks have all taken various measures to increase activities with greater profitability by seeking new clienteles and offering innovative products. Moreover, they have cut down on expenses by closing less profitable branches and cutting staff. As would have been expected, these activities and changes in government policies greatly improved the banks' profitability by 1987.

The commercial banks (a total of 29, many of which are subsidiaries of the three major banking groups mentioned earlier) provide all the customary banking services, merchant banking and underwriting services, and act as brokers on the Tel Aviv Stock Exchange. Through their subsidiaries and affiliates, they are engaged in mortgaging for building and development, development loans for industry and agriculture, loans for hotel and tourist development, municipal loans, leasing and hire purchase, and local and international credit cards. Other financial activities include the management of mutual trust, savings, provident and retirement funds, pension funds, security portfolios and employee-training funds, as well as insurance and real estate business.

Sources of short and long-term finance and access to venture capital are provided by the local banking system, although resources are scarce and the cost of money is high. Stringent liquidity requirements and a high degree of supervision by the Bank of Israel limit the volume of free credits available to the public. Consequently, funds are directed to help supply the essential finance for industrial development by way of industrial investment grants and relatively low interest loans.

Seven industrial, and three agricultural, development banks specialize in providing medium and long-term finance to industry, tourist and agricultural projects. The majority of funds are provided by the Treasury and channelled through these investment banks at subsidized interest rates, within the terms of the government's policy of encouraging investments. These banks serve as instruments for extending the government's financial assistance to "approved enterprises".

The Israeli banks have significant international activities and active correspondent relations with major foreign banks. In addition to its network of 320 branches throughout Israel, Bank Hapoalim, for example, operates 30 branches, subsidiaries and offices in the USA, South America, Canada, the UK and Europe. The bank maintains relationships with over 1000 correspondent banks in the world's major financial centers.

Abroad, the Israeli banks offer commercial banking, retail banking and foreign trade services with an emphasis on trade with Israel. Each bank has devised its own business strategy, with Bank Hapoalim, for example, seeking corporate business, and Bank Leumi concentrating on retail services. Private banking facilities is another area being developed by Bank Hapoalim for its clients around the world.

Israel's banking system plays an important role in the growth of its foreign trade. In the import of capital

Frenetic activity in Bank Hapoalim's head office dealing room.

The Stock Exchange is appropriately located in Tel Aviv, the financial center of the nation.

goods, for example, the international connections of Israel's banks enable them to offer clients medium-term credit lines obtained from financial institutions abroad. For exporters, all types of guarantees are offered — including bid-bond, performance and quality guarantees.

Full foreign currency services are also provided, with technologically advanced dealing rooms located in the head offices of the major Israeli banks. Forward deals, financial futures, interest rate swaps and all forms of foreign currency transactions are handled by Israel's banks on behalf of clients. Swift, Reuters systems and other advanced communications equipment enable the banks to carry out these transactions in real time.

Israel's banks are characterized by a high level of technological sophistication, enabling their clients in Israel to carry on many banking transactions at self-service terminals and to receive updated information on their accounts. A nationwide network of automatic teller machines services clients belonging to all the banks.

The Bank of Israel is the country's central bank, whose functions and powers are determined by law. Its primary functions are in the field of monetary policy, where it supervises and directs the funds made available as loans to the public. Among its other roles, the Bank of Israel maintains the country's foreign currency reserves and publishes a daily representative exchange rate of the shekel vis-a-vis the principal foreign currencies. The Bank of Israel regulates and supervises commercial and other banks, including their foreign activities, in order to ensure sound practices and to protect the public interest. It is also responsible for the availability of export finance and for foreign exchange control, while the Governor of the Bank acts as the government's official economic adviser.

Israel's capital market has been largely controlled by the government, which issues bonds, gives its approval to share and bond issues by other financial institutions, and determines the objectives of issues. A gradual deregulation and freeing of the capital market is now being planned, whereby firms will be able to, raise funds directly, or through financial institutions.

After a protracted three years' slump on the Tel Aviv Stock Exchange, a turning point in the securities market occurred in the middle of 1985. Accompanied by the government's economic stabilization program, the turnaround gained momentum in 1986 and the upward movement carried the market to new recovery highs by the end of spring, 1987.

In parallel to some of the world's fringe markets, such as Malaysia, Thailand and Taiwan, the performance of the Tel Aviv Stock Exchange in the first part of 1987 placed it on a par with the hottest stock market exchanges in the world. The bullish atmosphere on the TASE was a reflection of the new economic stability.

Many observers feel that the new driving force which may have a major influence over the development of the TASE until the end of the decade is the expected move by the Israeli government to initiate major changes in the Israeli capital market. These will include streamlining and simplifying procedures, with one of the goals being to make the country's capital market less dependent on the government. The other major anticipated trend is a government move to privatize many of its 250-plus state-owned corporations.

The first steps in the direction of privatization were experienced when 25 per cent of the share capital of the Jerusalem Economic Corporation was sold to the public. The issue was small, but it was vastly oversubscribed. The Israeli government is evaluating which of the companies in which it has an interest will be privatized. Optimists contend that privatization of "blue-chip" companies by way of the Stock Exchange could bring major economic benefits to Israel. The international search for global investments sees money moving rapidly from one country to another. The logic is that with billions of dollars seeking and focusing on investment opportunities in all parts of the world, it should be possible to attract funds. Even if only a small percentage were invested it would have a major impact.

"From the point of view of the Tel Aviv Stock Exchange, there is little difference whether shares are bought by Israelis or foreign residents. Of course, we would like to have more foreign participation", states Mr Haim Stoessel, chairman of the Exchange.

Foreign investors converting foreign currency into New Israeli Shekels in order to buy shares registered on the Tel Aviv Stock Exchange, are entitled when selling these securities to reconvert the proceeds at the existing rate of exchange, and to repatriate these funds and transfer them freely anywhere in the world.

"Our market has a potential for attracting foreign investments, just like any other market in the world", states Joseph Nitzani, general manager of TASE. "When the conditions are attractive, then money flows in. The question is: What kind of money? The cash received in 1982, at a time of prosperous stock market conditions, did not serve a constructive function. These were speculative funds which came into the country for short periods of time. The aim was to make a quick profit and then the money was withdrawn. There was little long-term investment money coming in. Economic stability is a precondition for the flow of money. Should the market awaken again, the influx of large sums of money is a very real possibility."

Haim Stoessel has mixed feelings about privatization. "I doubt whether the government would privatize, at one time, the largest of its holdings like the Paz Oil Company. The local market is still too small to absorb the shares of a company as large as Paz Oil." Expectations are that the government will initially offer, through the Stock Exchange, up to 25 per cent of its holdings in some of the country's larger concerns.

The TASE was founded in 1953. Ten years later, the Stock Exchange Clearing House Limited, which is fully controlled by the TASE, was established. As of the middle of 1987, the exchange membership included 16 banks, including the Bank of Israel, Israel's Central Bank and 11 non-banking members. It has 125 employees.

The professional term for the type of trading carried out in the TASE is the "call" market. In addition and on an experimental basis, continuous trading is carried out in 25 of the most liquid shares. The transactions carried out in the TASE include the purchase and sale of bonds, shares, warrants and convertible debentures. All the stock exchange transactions are for immediate settlement by way of the Stock Exchange Clearing House. The exchange is open from Sunday to Thursday with bonds being traded between 10.30 and 11.30am, while shares, warrants and convertible debentures are traded during two sessions, one from 9.00 to 11.30am

and the other one from 12.45 to 3.30pm.

The cost of transactions is competitive with a maximum of 1 per cent of transaction value being charge on the purchase or sale of shares and bonds. There is no minimum level and commissions of ¼ of 1 per cent are not uncommon on large transactions.

There is no capital gains tax levied on the sale of listed securities by individuals, other than dealers or professional traders. Income tax, at the rate of 35 per cent, is deducted at source, with some exceptions on interest and dividend payments. Generally, the 35 per cent deduction is considered final.

There is no limitation for foreigners to invest on the TASE. Foreign investors may buy or sell listed non-bank shares, as long as payment is executed by an authorized foreign exchange dealer, generally a bank. Interest and dividend payment and transfers, as well as capital repatriation, are payable at the then current exchange rate. The provision being that the securities were originally purchased against foreign currency. Foreign investors who wish to buy bonds or bank shares are not allowed to repatriate the funds invested.

The development of the price of the securities traded on the TASE is recorded by the general share index, which is compiled by the TASE on behalf of the Central Bureau of Statistics. It includes 19 sub-branch indices. There is also a general bond index with 16 sub-division indices.

As of June 30, 1987, the number of securities listed included 577 bonds series and 436 shares, warrants and convertible securities. The market value of the bonds and debentures as of June 30, 1987 stood at $7.7 million, while shares, warrants and convertibles had a market value of $11.3 billion.

In the first half of 1987, nine companies were listed for the first time, bringing up the total to 274. The value of stocks, warrants and convertible new issues in the first half of the year totalled $76 million. In the same period, the government floated $1.1 billion worth of bonds while other bond new listings accounted for $271 million. The total turnover of all securities traded on the TASE, in the first half of 1987, totalled $5.7 billion.

Investors and other interested parties wishing to obtain more information about the TASE, or updated 1988 figures, can obtain its publications, which include monthly and annual official lists and a stock and bond guide. The address to contact is: Public Relations Department, The Tel Aviv Stock Exchange, 54 Ahad Haam Street, Tel Aviv 65543, ISRAEL, P.O.B. 29060, Tel Aviv 61290, ISRAEL. Tel: 03-627411. Telex: 342112 TASE IL. □

Joseph Morgenstern is a leading international financial journalist based in Tel Aviv. He is the author of several books, gives frequent lectures, and writes a column for the Jerusalem Post.

The technology of tomorrow

In this article *Arnold Sherman* **focuses on developments in high technology industries in Tel Aviv and its environs.**

Having pioneered the applications of lasers for surgery, Laser Industries has now developed a new array of equipment for sensitive dental work.

TEL Aviv, a center for high technology? The statement would sound silly to most Israelis who are aware that modern electronics is, to a very large degree, centralized near Haifa and in the Galilee. And yet Tel Aviv plays two essential roles in the nation's onward thrust towards increasingly more sophisticated products and thus greater exports. It provides a haven for certain specialized industries which flourish in the city's characteristic environment, and offers an infrastructure for those enterprises located in other townships that still depend on the services and facilities of Israel's commercial hub. Tel Aviv's two universities, Tel Aviv and Bar-Ilan located between Jerusalem and Haifa, perform pure and applied research in dozens of areas which have commercial applications. They provide a highly intelligent reservoir of technically superior manpower which is attracted by the international flavor and cultural pursuits of the metropolis.

In particular, Israel has made major strides in medical technology. A combination of electronics and medicine, Israeli breakthroughs and products have been hailed throughout the world and have led to an entirely new range of investigations. One such area is the exciting new field of laser surgery, exemplified by Laser Industries Limited, which has subsidiaries and sales organizations throughout the United States and

Some companies would sell you a new pencil. We'd sell you a pencil sharpener.

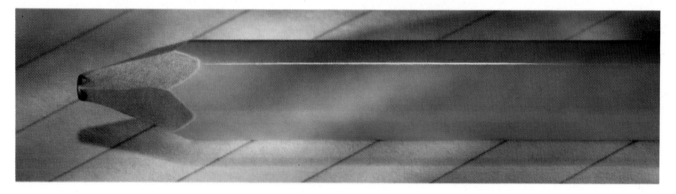

You could call it the NCR approach. We call it "Creating value."

It's based on a simple principle. One that applies as much to computers as it does to pencils.

Instead of making you buy computers that we want to make, we make computers that you want to buy.

Computers that talk to other computers.

Computers designed to do the job you want them to do.

Complete systems that are flexible enough to grow as your business grows.

Creating value. It's the whole point of our business.

To find out more, get in touch on (03) 209-511.

Creating value.

Europe, but is headquartered in Tel Aviv where the multi-million-dollar, multinational, multifaceted enterprise started. It all began simply enough in the early 1970s, when Professor Isaac Kaplan, one of Tel Aviv's leading plastic surgeons, visited the United States and witnessed early experiments employing CO_2 lasers to vaporize tissue.

In simple terms, a laser is a device emitting a beam of light focused with extremely high density of power on a small area. This characteristic allows lasers of certain wavelengths to be used as surgical tools to cut and vaporize tissues with precision. The laser beam is completely absorbed by water; the human tissue upon which it is focused is composed of between 70–90 per cent fluid. Thus the laser vaporizes the living tissue at its focal point while leaving adjacent areas virtually unaffected. Kaplan became an early convert to the laser, believing it could be transformed into an effective operating instrument, especially in problematical regions of the body. Imagination kindled, he considered its eventual usefulness in neurosurgery, burns treatment, plastic and reconstructive surgery, ear, nose and throat conditions, and orthopedic operations.

Kaplan quickly grasped the tremendous advantage of sealing while cutting. It meant reducing loss of blood, offering a dry operating area, greater sterility, with less pain and trauma for the person undergoing the operation. However, existing laser prototypes were unwieldy and awkward to use. Therefore, Kaplan decided to pursue the matter further with laser engineer Uzi Sharon. Financed by sympathetic entrepreneurs, they resolved to build a prototype more adapted to surgeons' specific needs. As a result, in 1972 the team produced its first clinical model which was then subjected to a year of testing and experimental operations. One year later, medical engineering leapfrogged into the future when the laser cutting tool was marketed by Laser Industries under the Sharplan trade name.

Administering an increasingly larger and more complex empire from Tel Aviv, the company is now the acknowledged world leader in the development, production and manufacture of carbon dioxide surgical lasers, accounting for the majority of CO_2 lasers sold in the United States every month. Sharplan lasers have several unique features, according to Laser Industries executive Shimshon Halperin. "They employ an extremely effective, patented, lightweight and maneuverable articulated arm and offer a combination of freehand and micro-surgery capabilities, and the possibility of switching rapidly between the two during operations. The company is now a leader in computerized laser surgery, a rapidly growing field, and in endoscopy."

The company's early shareholders were adventurous enough to invest millions of dollars in the development and marketing of Sharplan lasers during the seven years before the firm finally showed a profit in 1979. Because conservative physicians at the time resisted the new method, the firm tried to convert the skeptics by lending its lasers to hospitals for trial use.

Patience paid off. By the early 1980s sales were in excess of $12 million and were expanding by an additional 50 per cent each year. The Tel Aviv-based firm offers two basic models of surgical lasers for use in hospital operating rooms. It also produces smaller, mobile units for use in outpatient clinics, gynecological and skin treatment, and delicate eye surgery. More recently, a new opthalmic surgical laser was developed, and will sell for about one-third the price of other such tools on the market. Laser Industries have received American government approval to field-test the new device.

Halperin contended that his firm has only just begun to develop market potential. "There are still many uses for surgical lasers which have not been fully exploited. I believe that we have barely scratched the surface in terms of surgical possibilities. Most of the laser surgery done so far has been performed by specialists, whereas the greatest potential is with the general surgeon. I think it is only a matter of time before the medical and economic advantages become more widely recognized, and the use of lasers becomes more commonplace."

Another example of medical electronics nurtured and developed in Tel Aviv is in the increasingly important field of artificial organs. Artificial kidneys and dialysis machines continue to support innumerable victims of chronic renal failure. These patients must have their blood purified frequently, or they will be slowly poisoned by the excess water and wastes that their defective kidneys cannot process. Several Israeli firms have investigated ways of making life easier for kidney disease victims and for those who treat them. One problem was the restraint dialysis

PHOTO: LASER INDUSTRIES

Sharplan surgical lasers: the market is still expanding.

Based in Tel Aviv, Tadiran Israel Electronics is the country's largest electronics firm.

imposed on the patient's freedom and movement. Aiming to resolve this problem, Tel Aviv University researchers teamed up with a plastics company to develop a portable, artificial kidney for use in hospitals, home dialysis and while traveling. Weighing only 15 kilos, the unit is one the lightest dialysis machines ever invented — a definite coup for Tel Aviv research efforts.

Long before Israel was ever deemed a practical possibility, there were major Jewish efforts made to redeem the landscape which had been cruelly mutilated for millennia. Addressing itself to the specific problem of agriculture in Palestine, Jewish pioneers founded the Mikveh Israel Agricultural High School, just outside the present borders of Tel Aviv, at the end of the nineteenth century. Courses taught at the school dealt with finding the best varieties of seeds, animal husbandry and water management.

As a direct result of this pioneering research, which was further pursued by the Volcani Institute in Rehovot, the Technion's Department of Agricultural Engineering in Haifa, and the Ben-Gurion University of the Negev, the amount of land under irrigation increased dramatically in the 40 years following the establishment of Israel. A desert which once lapped at the very doorstep of Tel Aviv has been banished to well beyond the Negev capital of Beersheva, nearly 130 kilometers to the south. Fruit and vegetables have been coaxed to grow throughout the year following land redemption and the application of new hothouse techniques.

Israel soon startled the world in the fields of husbandry and poultry. Its chickens laid more eggs and its cows produced more milk than anywhere else in the world. Even the petrified desert landscape adjacent to the Dead Sea was partially reclaimed, with winter vegetables and dates growing in an area previously deemed hopelessly dead by British agricultural ex-

perts during the Mandate.

Work also continues to include new Tel Aviv University research facilities for collecting the genetic materials of wild oats, barley and wheat. Having originated in the Middle East and evolved for millennia, these grains developed natural resistance to disease and pests and a better balance in protein and unsaturated oil. Professor Isaac Wahl, founder and director of Tel Aviv University's Institute for Cereal Crops Improvement, has used this priceless natural resource to enrich the genetic material of cultivated crops for several decades. These enhanced wild grain materials were disseminated and adopted in 30 different countries through the United States Department of Agriculture, the United Nations and other international organizations. Over 35 per cent of the oat acreage in the United States stems from this material, providing excellent protection against certain previously devastating diseases. The wheat, barley and oat material widely distributed after rigorous testing for quality and for disease resistance improved cereals the world over — with cultivated crops more resistant to disease, yet nutritionally superior. Stated Professor Wahl: "Today's food is provided by only 15 species of plants, representing a very narrow and limited genetic base. Of these, some of the better varieties extend over vast areas and may be wiped out entirely if a new dangerous pathogen appears. Cereal crops are genetically too uniform and dangerously subject to vast damage."

While other cereal banks exist for cultivated crops, the Middle East — the cradle of wild cereal crops — offers a wealth of genetic material which has yet to be collected and applied to the task of conquering hunger. Towards this end, the pioneering work of Tel Aviv University has established a vital scientific momentum.

Israel is a world leader in computer application for classrooms, boasting that between 40 and 50 per cent of all primary school children now receive this special training. Eight thousand youngsters use computer-aided instruction (CAI) systems for arithmetic, reading comprehension, English as a second language, typing and programming.

The largest high-tech firm in the field, Degem Systems Limited, with computer products for CAI, high-tech training systems, military technological training, skills development, rural development and agricultural training, is another proud resident of Tel Aviv. Degem markets computer-aided testing and practice systems for classrooms as a complete educational package, including equipment, programs, educational material, teacher training, installation, maintenance, control and expert support. The system can handle up to 1400 students, in all grades, depending on utilization and scheduling. For example, if arithmetic is the only subject in the current program, 1400 pupils can drill twice a week (the standard requirement) in 20-minute sessions.

Computer work is divided into two stages. The testing stage consists of 12 10-minute lessons at the terminal. The pupil begins at a relatively low level in order to adjust to the keyboard, to reading instructions on the screen, and to the system's work procedures. As he grows more comfortable with the system, the exercise level is lowered or raised until he can do two-thirds of the exercises correctly.

In the second stage, the practice stage, the student does various exercises on different topics. Success in each topic is recorded separately. The exercises match the student's current level in each specific topic. Once proficient, he moves up to the next level. Otherwise he remains at the same level, or is moved down to a lower one. Each lesson continues from where the previous one finished. Movement between levels is fully automatic and the pupil does not know he is being moved up or down. The teacher receives a detailed weekly report of the student's performance and plans classroom activities accordingly.

With bases in 60 countries on five continents, a worldwide service network and 15 years' experience, Degem maintains a close relationship with its clients. As a result, the Tel Aviv firm has been able to expand into related fields; for example, it has earned a worldwide reputation for military training systems.

Thanks to its experience and support facilities, Degem can both design and implement CAI systems nationwide. Even the education ministries of underdeveloped countries can employ the same methods that succeeded in raising educational levels in Israel's development towns. The Degem system includes a Project Center to coordinate and supervise the system nationally, so teachers and computer experts can determine how, when and where to implement new courseware. Several regional centers coordinate activity between schools and the Project Center.

Degem markets mobile CAI classrooms for sparsely populated regions and areas where budgets are limited and CAI facilities must be shared by several schools or communities. The mobile classrooms require no advance site preparation and reduce overheads considerably.

There are many other interesting high technology developments around Tel Aviv. The expansion of the local microelectronics industry, for example, gave Israel the capacity to produce the chip — the heart of the computer — from design to production, start to finish. Motorola, the giant American corporation, officially inaugurated its five-million-dollar chip design center in Ramat Gan in December, 1984. Why set up the center in Israel and why locate to the Tel Aviv area? Motorola World Vice President Murray Goldman explained: "To be competitive in the world market we have to have the very best people working on our products and our experience in Israel has been very positive over the past 20 years. Israel has the creative people we needed to work on this very high technology product."

Also based in Tel Aviv, the country's largest electronics firm, Tadiran Israel Electronics Limited, has placed strong emphasis on research and development, along with purchase and development of advanced technologies. It designs and produces civilian products and plays an essential role in military electronics.

Itzhak Ish-Hurvitz, who has held several senior positions at Tadiran and is a graduate of both the Technion and the Harvard Business School, explained, "Not only in electronics, but in all technologically intensive fields, Tadiran must move into areas that change rapidly. We must select those niches where technological changes take place very often. The selection and solution of these problems are within our capabilities, while exploiting resources like raw materials and cheap labor is not. We can compete if the name of the game is innovation, creativity, new technologies."

Reflecting the fortunes of the industry as a whole, Tadiran grew from a modest company producing consumer goods alone in the 1960s to an electronics conglomerate with a wide range of products, a work force of thousands and a turnover of millions in the 1980s. Founded in 1961, the firm comprises five separate divisions — military communications, electronics systems, telecommunications, industrial and electric equipment, and consumer goods. Its products comprise basic components like printed circuit boards and batteries, civilian communications systems and a wide range of military equipment such as its very successful remotely piloted vehicle (RPV) used in the 1982 war in Lebanon and then translated into a hot export item.

Tel Aviv and its suburbs consist of more than just coffee houses, theaters and good restaurants. It is one of *the* high technology centers in the country, prodding and developing new research that will eventually be the cornerstone of Israel's economy. ☐

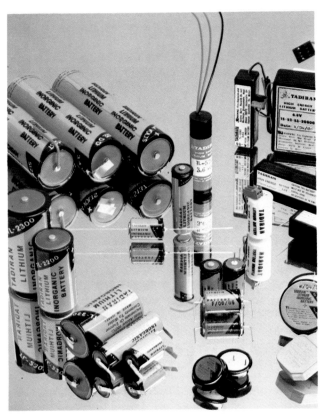

Tadiran's battery range.

Keeping up the commerce

Starting from an exportless and non-industrial economy, Israel has become, in the space of just 40 years, a modern state with annual exports worth over $10 billion.

Tel Aviv-Jaffa's Chamber of **Commerce is a key element in the business and commercial life of the city.** *Kenneth L Fischer* **has a penetrating look at the subject.**

WITH almost one-quarter of Israel's population, Tel Aviv and its suburbs is the country's center of commerce. The main offices of the country's banks, manufacturing and commercial companies, exporters, importers, and others are located there. Tel Aviv is also the chief retailing center for the entire country.

This conglomerate of business and commercial interests is served today by the Tel Aviv-Jaffa Chamber of Commerce which, among other things, represents and safeguards these interests in dealing with government and public institutions and renders various services to individuals and companies aimed at furthering their economic and professional interests. The Chamber of Commerce has set up the professional systems for gathering and sorting of information, and employs a team of highly qualified experts who are available to consult the firms and individuals on a broad range of subjects. Its professional publications contain useful information for the business community and up-to-date data and statistics in all areas vital to business. It also engages in activities which are meant to create and foster commercial ties in import and export through trade-related services, and by supporting projects aimed at assisting deals in the business sector.

Today the Chamber of Commerce is an automonous body, free of dependence upon the government or any other institution. It is democratically managed by a presidium and an elected council, and its budget is financed by membership fees from companies and individuals, and from various services provided to the public.

But it was not always so. The whole thing started back in 1919 under British rule, when a brigadier was assigned to set up what was then the Office of Commercial Services for Palestine. It was located in Jaffa, and served both Jews and the Arabs until 1921, when riots forced the opening of separate offices — one for the Arabs in Jaffa, and the Jewish one in Tel Aviv.

Before becoming the first mayor of Tel Aviv, Meir Dizengoff was director of the commercial secretariat following the 1948 War of Independence and the closing of the Jaffa office. He was followed in this position by A Z Hofian, who expanded development greatly, pushing through such projects as the Port of Tel Aviv, the Israel Trade Fair Center (which was at first located within the city, and which now has its own spacious grounds north of the city), and the Israel Convention Center. In addition to its commercial activities, the office was also responsible for providing the food convoys to Jerusalem.

In the years since the establishment of the state, Israeli society and its economy have gone through many changes. Starting with a population of 600 000 with hardly any industry and no exports, within 40 years Israel has developed into a state with a population approaching five million and a modern sophisticated economy whose annual exports approach $10 billion. The process of transforming a handful of refugees from 70 countries into an advanced nation employing modern social and economic methods was not easy. Indeed, the process is still underway, and the country is constantly faced with difficulties and problems to be solved — not least in the area of economics. Israel today is a country which can take pride in its highly sophisticated technology, and whose infrastructure and commercial system, while well developed, have great potential for developing further.

The Chamber of Commerce is an integral part of this process as a representative of the business/commercial sector and as a representative of free enterprise interests. All its workers and officers wear two hats — one as staff for the Tel Aviv-Jaffa Chamber of Commerce, and the other for the Israeli Federation of Chambers of Commerce. The Tel Aviv unit functions through several bodies.

The Presidium and Council are its elected bodies, with the Council determining the Chamber's policies, and the Presidium, headed by President Dan Gillerman, supervising its performance.

There are about 50 professional trade sections, each headed by an elected committee which sets the guidelines for its operation. The section coordinator, a Chamber employee, carries out the operations. These sections deal with professionally related problems encountered by members, whether among themselves, or in their contacts with government authorities.

The Chamber of Commerce provides its members with a wide range of advisory services, employing experts from its own ranks as well as from outside, who cover the following subjects: economics, taxation, labor and wages, import, finances, standardization, foreign currency risks and commodity future trading, shipping by sea and air, maritime insurance, marketing, packaging, conveyance and transportation, documentation, and international trade procedures.

Since the size of its business/commercial community is so large relative to those in other Israeli cities, the Tel Aviv-Jaffa Chamber of Commerce also represents the Israeli Federation of Chambers of Commerce. This is the unifying body for the Chambers of Commerce of Tel Aviv, Jerusalem, Haifa, Beersheva, and Nazareth. The Chamber and Federation often take economic initiatives and present programs and proposals for new legislation concerning the economy. These proposals are submitted to government ministers and senior civil servants, and are analyzed at meetings attended by government ministers, members of the Knesset, and prominent economists.

An example of a specific proposal by the Chamber of Commerce which was adopted as amended, is the "Proposal for reform of the Israeli tax system." After careful and expert consideration within the Chamber, this proposal in its entirety was submitted to Shimon Peres, then Prime Minister, and the Minister of Finance in August 1986. At the same time, it was brought to public discussion through meetings, publication of position papers, conferences with the news media, and release to the US Embassy. After due deliberation and with some amendments, in January 1987, the Treasury accepted what was mainly the Chamber's proposal. Implementation of the reforms began, and some beneficial effects are already filtering into the economy.

With Tel Aviv-Jaffa commerce burgeoning, the business body has now moved into areas such as ocean port, sea transport, and customs and taxes — lobbying in the Knesset and Histadrut for suggestions. With its national perspective, the Chamber is in the process of initiating several imaginative programs for the benefit of its members:

- Establishment of a business information center, which will include investment opportunities and commercial contacts
- Establishment of a small business administration to provide members with an opportunity for entrepreneurship. Here they will find assistance from lawyers, help for registering in and entering the stock market, training in business operation, and 10 to 20-year state loans up to $50 000. Grants for new product development will also be made available, with the money to come from the state, the banks, and the Chamber of Commerce itself
- Creation of a board of arbitration at the Chamber of Commerce. This will substitute for the courts where possible, providing an informal atmosphere, saving time as well as court and legal fees
- A Marketing Institute for the advancement and improvement of marketing within Israel.

From its vantage point on the commercial high ground of Tel Aviv, the Chamber of Commerce with its broad view and statesmanlike outlook has been a key to the domestic and international advancement of Israel's business and commerce. Its invaluable assistance will continue to play a part in the whole country's development — and that of the city it represents so admirably. □

Kenneth L. Fischer moved to Israel in the 1960s and settled in the fishing moshav of Michmoret, where he has been reporting on industrial topics for many years.

Academic tradition

Tel Aviv University and Bar-Ilan give Tel Aviv-Jaffa a profound sense of intellectual achievement reflected not only in academia, but in cultural pursuits, according to *Gordon Shifman.*

Tel Aviv University is the pride of the city, performing invaluable research and catering to tens of thousands of graduate and post graduate students from Israel and abroad.

flourishes

GREATER Tel Aviv's 30 000-plus student population permeates the entire cultural fabric of the metropolis and its suburbs. The urban sprawl may seem far removed from the elegance of the academic world, but this has not prevented the area's student body from achieving the critical mass necessary to make itself felt in every form of local cultural activity. Israeli students, who have mostly completed regular army service, generally maintain a lower profile than their foreign counterparts. But they still lend an essential touch of youthful, stimulating spirit to the sidewalk cafés, cinemas, concert halls and theaters of Israel's cultural capital. Anyone who fails to grasp the exciting student spirit of Tel Aviv will at least acknowledge the strikingly attractive architecture of its two university campuses — Tel Aviv and Bar-Ilan.

Tel Aviv University, located in the northern suburb of Ramat Aviv, has the distinction of being the world's largest Jewish university. It has 20 000 full-time under-graduate and graduate students and a further 9000 students enrolled in extramural studies and other non-degree programs. The more homely sized Bar-Ilan University, located on the eastern periphery of Ramat Gan, claims another distinction as the most Jewish of Israel's universities. In fact, both institutions are as deeply involved in Judaism as they are with the universal world of academic study and research.

Tel Aviv University was founded as a municipal institution in 1953, when the need for higher educatio-nal facilities was growing in pace with the city's rapid expansion. Beginning with the University Institute of Natural Sciences, it later incorporated the Tel Aviv School of Law and Economics (established in 1935) and the Institute of Jewish Studies, becoming an autonomous government-funded university institu-tion in 1956.

The 200-acre Ramat Aviv campus was opened in 1964. This is one of the major sights of Tel Aviv, and not simply because of its attractive modern architecture and liberal expanses of greenery. Within its bound-aries is the Bet Hatefutsot Museum of the Jewish Diaspora — a must on any tourist's itinerary — containing a wealth of displays on the life of the Jews in all the lands of their dispersion. The University's Botanical Gardens hold a rich variety of plant life, a welcome attraction in any big city, while the Canadian Center for Ecological Zoology specializes in animals indigenous to Israel — some of them almost extinct — and has the world's largest collection of Middle Eastern fauna. The university also operates Israel's only astronomical observatory.

Nine faculties and 75 research institutes housed on the campus cover a wide range of academic studies: Engineering, Exact Sciences, Humanities, Law, Life Sciences, Management, Social Sciences, Visual and Performing Arts — including an academy of music — and Medicine, which includes dental medicine.

During its three decades of existence, Tel Aviv University has built up a worldwide academic reputa-tion and regularly hosts international conferences and symposia. It also maintains academic exchange agree-ments and conducts joint research projects with all of the western world's major educational institutions. The university receives financial support in the form of research grants from the Ford Foundation, the Nation-al Aeronautics and Space Administration (NASA), the Rothschild Foundation, the US Armed Forces, the US National Science Foundation, the American National Cancer Institute and even the UN.

In the international arena, Tel Aviv University's Dayan Center for Middle Eastern and African Studies provides a major source of information on what is certainly, and unfortunately, likely to remain one of the world's most politically volatile regions. The Center regularly publishes in-depth studies of the political, economic, social and cultural aspects of Israel's neigh-bors. And on military and strategic issues, the universi-ty's Jaffee Center for Strategic Studies constitutes an independent think-tank advising Israeli policymakers and overseas observers on Middle Eastern and world-wide security matters. The authoritative *Middle East Military Balance* has been published annually by the center since 1983. It includes reviews of strategic developments in the region, a lengthy inventory of its armed forces, and analyses of various local conflicts, such as Israel-Syria and Iran-Iraq. The think-tank also compiles studies on the worldwide effect of changes in Middle East oil prices, the enroachment of Islamic fundamentalism, and international terrorism emanat-ing from the Middle East.

Tel Aviv University's medical faculty is the largest in Israel and is affiliated to 13 hospitals in and around the metropolis, including three major ones, Ichilov, Beilin-son and Sheba, which is in Tel Hashomer. This

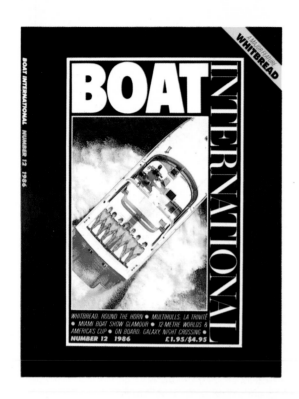 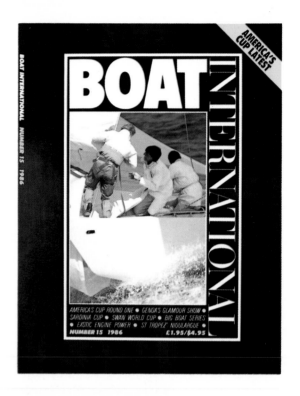

FOR THE CONNOISSEUR

Yachting has never looked better

The modern campus at Tel Aviv University.

involvement in the country's health services extends to its post-1967 boundaries. For the past two years, the university has run a postgraduate course in internal medicine for Arab doctors from the West Bank to familiarize physicians with the latest developments in internal medicine, while promoting cooperation between Jews and Arabs in the field of public health. The medical faculty is now exploring the possibility of establishing a postgraduate school for West Bank and Gaza doctors, nurses, physiotherapists, technicans and speech therapists.

Applied research at the medical faculty has a considerable impact on medical and dental care throughout the country, as well as abroad. A recent example of this is the non-operative treatment of prostate gland disorders. Affected tissues are heated with an instrument called a "Prostatherma", now produced by Biodan Medical Systems Limited and designed by Tel Aviv University and Weizmann Institute medical researchers. Unlike conventional prostate therapy, which almost always involves surgery, treatment using this instrument requires no hospitalization or even sedation and promises to offer a far less traumatic form of relief for the large proportion of adult males who are likely to suffer from prostate trouble at some time in their lives.

While the medical faculty is taking the pain out of prostate treatment, dentists, psychiatrists and psychologists working at its dental school have recently developed a form of relaxation therapy at a clinic within the school, to help patients who are terrified of sitting in the dentist's chair. Anyone who thinks this is just a case of mollycoddling the squeamish should remember that there are people who are allergic to local anaesthetics!

After Tel Aviv was officially accorded university status in 1956, the first new faculty to be opened was the Recanati School of Business Administration. Now considered one of the world's top 10 business schools, it works in close cooperation with, and as part of

Israel's business leadership. Every month the school hosts a financial club where the country's leading industrialists and businessmen are invited to exchange ideas with each other and with faculty staff. Internationally coordinated projects are carried out with the University of Pennsylvania's Wharton School of Finance and Commerce, allowing Tel Aviv students to take a very active role in Israel's industrial development. In this project, six selected Israeli are examined by marketing students who develop export plans for the companies' products, allowing the students to gain substantial practical experience at an early stage in their careers.

Although Bar-Ilan is regarded as Israel's bastion of academic Jewish studies, these are far from neglected at Tel Aviv University. The Chaim Rosenberg School of Jewish Studies is involved in all aspects of Judaica, including the history of Zionism, and is devoted to safeguarding the legacies of Jewish cultural heritage. Recalling Jewish history's darkest hours, the university's Wiener Library houses the world's largest collection of books on anti-semitism and the Holocaust.

One year older than Tel Aviv University and located off Israel's busiest north-south highway, Bar-Ilan projects the peculiarly scholastic tranquility of long-established European seats of learning. This is probably the result of a largely successful attempt to incorporate the tradition of an ancient, in this case Jewish, culture into a modern university. For however many resources are devoted by Israel's other universities to Jewish studies, they are all essentially secular institutions whose student bodies occasionally reject their own cultural heritage. Not so Bar-Ilan: in the words of its Chancellor, Professor Emanuel Rackman, this university has the mission of "holding the center".

Bar-Ilan provides a vital link between the secular and Orthodox sectors of Israeli society. To this end, the university's courses are geared to integrating the most stimulating aspects of Jewish studies with secular subjects. Unlike any other Israeli university, Bar-Ilan requires all of its students, regardless of their area of specialization, to devote 25 per cent of their curriculum to Judaic topics. Study options include the Old Testament, Talmud, Jewish history, Hebrew and Semitic languages and the literature of the Jewish people.

The resulting academic environment makes Bar-Ilan the only major institute of learning in the Jewish world where an almost equal proportion of religious and non-religious students fraternize and study together. As a result Bar-Ilan has students identifying with every shade of the political spectrum. The policy line promulgated by faculty heads is described as "centrist Orthodox" — that is, they are opposed to extremism of the right and left, as well as to extremists of the ultra-Orthodox or the ultra-secular sections of Israeli society.

The university was established in 1955 and named after Rabbi Meir Bar-Ilan, a scholar with a solid reputation with the nation's religious and secular communities. The 8000-strong student body is divided into 40 separate departments within five major faculties: Jewish Studies, Humanities, Social Sciences, Natural Sciences and Mathematics and Law. A further 2500 students are enrolled in special courses and programs designed to cater for every adult age group and sector of Israeli society. Extramural students attend the university's branch courses in Safed, Tzemah (in the Jordan Valley) and Ashqelon, and 1200 pensioners registered with a special program attend regular classes as well as their own specific courses. Having operated for over a decade, this enlightened project is the first of its kind in an Israeli educational institution. Apart from the direct benefit derived by the pensioners, the program is a highly successful experiment in intergenerational communication and serves as a model which other universities hope to emulate.

The ratio of religious to non-religious students at Bar-Ilan is 60:40. To attract enrolment from the country's development towns, whose populations originate mainly from Arab countries, the proportion of Oriental Jewish students, standing at 34 per cent, is the highest of any Israeli university. Because of its religious environment, it also attracts young women from Orthodox homes who would not usually attend university at all, and yeshiva graduates wanting to broaden their education without leaving an Orthodox milieu.

Bar-Ilan's prestigious Faculty of Law reflects the university's abhorrence of religious isolationism by advocating the redemption of Jewish Law (Mishpat Ivri) in civil, criminal and public jurisprudence. Strongly supporting the revival of Jewish Law, Rackman has said "The revival of Hebrew, the historic language, contributed much to national unity in the rebirth of the State and all that preceded it. The revival of the historic jurisprudence can make a similar contribution to national unity and while some Jews will continue to study that part of Jewish law which deals with faith and practices for their personal guidance and spiritual edification, the other part which deals with civil, criminal and public law can be linked with new developments and thus there will be continuity from Abraham and Moses down to the ever-changing present. They also seek this result because it is one of the best ways to make preoccupation with Jewish law relevant to the contemporary scene."

Rackman continues with an oblique reference to religious isolationists: "Otherwise, the study of Talmud and Codes becomes an academic discipline serving no practical purpose."

Bar-Ilan is, in fact, already helping to apply Jewish law in contemporary legal practice by combining modern science and ancient Jewish learning. In this most interesting project, called Responsa, the university's Institute for Information Data Retrieval and Computational Linguistics programmed an IBM 3081 computer (which serves the university's departments) with written questions and answers on religious matters, as well as the Old Testament and the 36-volume Babylonian Talmud. As a result, several hundred legal opinions based on Responsa computer citations have been provided for Israeli judges and lawyers by a special Hebrew law team working within the framework of the institute's service unit. Precedents from Jewish law, and not only from secular codes, have been admissible in Israeli civil courts since the early 1980s; jurists searching for precedents in Hebrew law now have ready access to extensive source material on criminal, civil and domestic relations litigation, as well as summary opinions on which they can base their pleadings in court. Until the Responsa Project was completed in 1985, scholars and rabbis often had to spend days sifting through some half a million questions and answers to clarify a particular issue of Talmudic law, a process which can now be completed within minutes.

In the scientific field, more than 300 research projects are currently being conducted at Bar-Ilan. The university's Health Sciences Research Center undertakes major research projects on male fertility, the use of lymphokines in retarding cancer growth, the relationship between metabolism of glucose and muscular dystrophy, and the development of antioxidants to combat the aging process. A research team at Bar-Ilan headed by Dr Michael Albeck, rector of the university, and Dr Benjamin Sredni, associate professor of Life Sciences, has recently developed a drug, AS101, which stimulates the body's immune system. This drug has been used to treat various forms of cancer and may be able to offer some degree of relief to AIDS sufferers.

As with AS101, which is produced by Scientific Testing Inc, a joint venture formed by Bar-Ilan and a New York company, the university sells new products and processes arising out of successful research projects to US firms. The ensuing royalties provide the university with much-needed financial support to counterbalance cuts in the government's education budget. □

Gordon Shifman is a well-known Tel Aviv—based journalist and translator who writes extensively about higher education in Israel.